Praying a Blessing for Someone

Why waste your time worrying for a loved one, when you could spend that same time praying powerful prayers of salvation, breakthrough, and blessings instead? Join Eric Sprinkle and Laura Shaffer as they give you the blueprint for prayers that make a world of difference.

> Linda Evans Shepherd, bestselling author of *Praying God's Promises* and *Praying Through Every Emotion*

Praying for Someone's Salvation

Thoroughly comprehensive, practical, clear, inspiring and helpful. HIGHLY recommend.
Laura Shaffer along with Eric Sprinkle, has used her gentle, comprehensive and long-ranging experience of intercessory prayer to compose a guiding book which is user-friendly, encouraging and hope-inspiring. Hang on in there. Keep praying.

> Early Amazon Reviewer

I like this book because the prayers are sooo much more powerful and give me ideas on what words to use through the day. See, I'm 8 1/2 and my friends at school do not know Jesus. This helps me focus.

> Amazon Reviewer (with Mom)

I've been doing the *40 Day Prayer Guides—Praying for Someone's Salvation* for about 2 weeks now and it's such a huge blessing. The prayers are wonderful, and working through each day's prayers has definitely been a blessing to me each morning. I am actively seeking time with the person I am praying for as a result of praying for him and we have had a lot of fun... plus it has laid a groundwork of trust for God to work in through our conversations.

> Robin Shear, professional Joy Coach, author of the JOY BITES blog & an upcoming book about finding joy despite difficult circumstances. (www.joytotheworldcoaching.com)

Praying for Godly Character

"Are you ready for a real adventure? Ignite your prayer life with this 40-Day guide and see what God will do!"

> Award-winning author Amy Robnik Joob

Praise for the 40 Day Prayer Guide series

You two make such a great team. Not only is Laura's content rich and practical, but Eric's photos also add a powerful and needed dimension to the prayers. Well done!

> Dick Bruso, Branding/Marketing Expert and Founder of "Heard Above The Noise"

You can pick up this book and begin praying immediately because the prayers are right there for you. Laura guides us as a "prayer warrior," sharing her words and letting us make them our own. Thanks to this book, applying prayer is easier than ever before."

> Laine Lawson Craft, best-selling author of *Enjoy Today Own Tomorrow*

I love the images and photos in these books. They are such an inspiration! Some of them excite me, others spark my imagination. And sometimes, one of them will completely transport me away to another place. A beautiful, quiet place, far away from life's stresses, where I can sit for a minute, reflecting on God's goodness, and on my wonderful prayer time with Him.

> Susan Neal, RN, MBA, MHA Director, Christian Indie Publishers Association, and best-selling author of *7 Steps to Get Off Sugar and Carbohydrates*

40 DAY PRAYER GUIDES

Praying for Your Grandchild

Powerful day-by-day Prayers Inviting God to Encourage and Shape Their Lives

Eric Sprinkle and Laura Shaffer

Praying for Your Grandchild, Powerful day-by-day Prayers Inviting God to Encourage and Shape Their Lives

All photos by Eric Sprinkle
Cover and interior design by Robin Black

ISBN: 978-1-7322694-5-3

Published by Adventure Experience Press in partnership with the fine folks at
EA Books Books Publishing, a division of
Living Parables of Central Florida, Inc. a 501c3

AdventureExperience.net
EABooksPublishing.com

DEDICATIONS

Laura

To my grandparents HC and Odessa Fail, and DW and my Minnie Gray
who knew and loved the Lord. They taught me to love God,
love my country, and love my family. I am who I am
because of their love and encouragement.
To my parents Tom and Truda Fail and my husband's parents
Larry and Francis Shaffer, who were amazing grandparents
and filled my sons' lives with love, hugs,
and more sugar than was necessary.
And to Anfisa, who is 2 and Logan who is 13 and any and all other
grandchildren who I am blessed to have come into my life.

Eric

To grandparents Sprinkle and Morris,
Between the farm animals, the apple orchard, and the amazing
Christmas cookies, you all definitely created some amazing childhood
memories for me. As I chase adventures today, there's always a small
part of me still jumping across that old creek behind the farmhouse;
chasing crayfish, being fascinated by frogs, and swinging
around on some really sketchy vines and tree limbs.
Forgive the muddy shoes, but childhood was a blast because of it.

ACKNOWLEDGEMENTS

- Robin, Rebecca, and the Team at EA Books for once again helping us create, format, and put this book together.
- Tim Shoemaker, it was a chilly Nov afternoon just last year when you brought up the idea for this book over lunchtime deep dish Chicago-style pizza. Ten months later, look at it now! Thanks much for being the inspiration for it all...and the pizza was amazing.
- Debbie "Fabulous" Hardy, Editor and lover of Mimi's five-cheese grilled cheese sandwich and French onion soup.
- I owe a debt of gratitude to my amazing prayer partners over the years who have been a blessing in my life, teaching me how to pray by example through our Torah group, Moms in Prayer groups, Community groups, and Bible studies. Their prayers and encouragement are invaluable.
- Extra special thanks go to the experienced grandmothers who have taken part in our "Becoming a Grandmother" Showers over the years! To Cathy, Cyndie, Jan, Marilyn, Suzanne, Beth, Melissa, Linda, Vera, Carol, Bette: Thank you! Your gifts, collective wisdom, and prayers continue to be invaluable.
- Last and always, to our Gracious Lord God, who not only hears our prayers and closely watches over children, but also blesses us far beyond what we could ever dare to ask or even hope to imagine.

Soli Deo Gloria indeed.

INTRODUCTION TO 40 DAYS

Let's face it, our gracious Lord God has a thing for 40 days. Forty days of rain to flood the earth, 40 days before the clock ran down on Nineveh to return to Him, 40 days spent in the wilderness before Jesus started his ministry. Over and over, we see 40 days as the time frame God uses for major changes in people and circumstances.

Now, there's a good chance you're already praying for your grandkids, but what if we changed it up a bit? What if we prayed for them, and for you, the grandparents, for the next 40 days?

Maybe this could be a time for God to bless them in ways you never thought of before. Like with sleep, bullies, and developing their work ethic. Asking God to shape their heart so that they would honor life—both their own and all others. And how about fanning the flames of your own memories of your grandparents? How they impacted you, in ways big and small, and how you can now turn that into something special for them.

And we'll start it all off with a 40 day prayer journey.

God loves it when we talk to and share with Him through prayer. Share our thoughts, our fears, our celebrations, and concerns. The Bible tells us it's our prayers and petitions, with thanksgiving, that God uses to bring us peace (Phil 4:6-7). Jesus himself told the disciples that sometimes when casting out demons only prayer will do the trick (Mark 9:29).

Maybe it's just me, but I get the feeling that I've vastly underestimated just how powerful prayer can be—and maybe you've felt that way too.

So, let's change it up. Let's make beautiful, Bible-based, laser-focused prayers a part of our daily routine for the next 40 days. Prayers for either one-grandkid-at-a-time, or all at once. And instead of trying to think of the words, we'll use some wonderful, powerful, stirring prayers from your new friend Laura.

Let's read her prayers and make them our own. Let's pray them silently or aloud, inserting the name(s) of the kiddos along the way. Don't worry, it'll be almost automatic by the time you get to Day 4.

What if we add a second grandchild to pray for? What if we invite someone else to pray with us too? What if 'GramGram' and 'Paw Paw' go on this 40 day journey together? Every morning over coffee, lifting up the same grandkids, asking together for our gracious Heavenly Father to impact their young lives. To reveal Himself. To call them to Him. To bless them with safety, direction, and a saving knowledge of Our Lord God.

Our Heavenly Father loves hearing our requests to Him through prayer. He loves blessing us with gifts too, often far more than we could ever ask or imagine.

So I wonder what He wants to do in the lives of your grandkids?

I say we find out.

It's time to turn the page and begin a 40 day journey, focused on praying blessing all over those special little kiddos, one that's going to impact them, and you as well.

Are you ready?

Let's do this.

Introduction to Praying for your Grandchild

However they come to you...natural, adoption, blended family, planned, unplanned, convenient, inconvenient, newborn or any other age, healthy or with challenges and special needs, they are your grandchild.

Grandchildren are a gift! They will need and benefit from your love and involvement in their life. And you, theirs.

If you are fortunate enough to live near them and can spend time with them in person, how wonderful! It will afford you opportunities to do things together and share life face to face.

If you live farther away, your communications and interactions may be through Facetime, Zoom, phone, text, or by cards and letters.

No matter the distance or state of the relationship, prayer is a gift you can give your grandchild and their parents. This book will guide you through 40 prayers to bless you and your grandchild. They can be prayed as they are or can act as a springboard to inspire your own prayers.

And if you miss a day you can just start from where you left off whenever you can.

At the end of each week of daily prayers there is a Reflect, Show and Share section. We hope it will give you ideas for ways to connect with your grandchild or spur your own imagination for new ideas. Or perhaps help you recall memories you have of your own grandparents.

And Appendix Resource pages provide prayers you can pray as your grandchild passes through different stages. And more!

In choosing this book for yourself or as a gift, I have prayed this blessing over each reader:

> May the God of peace bring you peace and equip you with all goodness and kindness to do His will as you love and care for this precious little one and their family.
>
> May the Lord increase your love for this child and their family regardless of the circumstances of how they came to you.
>
> May the Lord spread his protection over this child and their family, and you as you interact with them; over body, mind and spirit.
>
> May God strengthen you when you need the energy, stamina, patience, or wisdom to be there and care for your grandchild.

As you love and serve, may you see that love returned to you through your grandchild and family.

May God give you words that are full of grace, and boldness to speak of His love for your grandchild and to fearlessly proclaim the Gospel to future generations. Amen

Foreword

"They don't have a prayer." How many times have we heard that expression of speech? And if you're referring to an opposing team—or some ridiculous goal, it may be appropriate.

But when people refer to our grandkids' generation with a "they-don't-have-a-prayer" attitude? That's tragic.

Sure. Our grandkids face some massive challenges. Screen addictions. Depression. Churches that have strayed from the truth of God's Word. Parents who are preoccupied, self-absorbed—or failing to live out their faith. Our grandkids live in a culture that is increasingly hostile to Christians. But there must be something we can do to help our grandkids, right?

In 2 Kings 20, King Hezekiah was ill and was told by the prophet Isaiah that he was going to die. Hezekiah prayed earnestly. He wept. And God heard him, granting Hezekiah fifteen more years of life.

Shortly after his recovery, envoys from Babylon visited Hezekiah. The king made a huge mistake—and gave them a proud tour of the nation's treasures. Isaiah confronted Hezekiah.

> *"Then Isaiah said to Hezekiah, 'Hear the word of the LORD: The time will surely come when everything in your palace, and all that your fathers have stored up until this day, will be carried off to Babylon. Nothing will be left, says the LORD. And some of your descendants, your own flesh and blood, that will be born to you, will be taken away and they will become eunuchs in the palace of the king of Babylon.'*
>
> *"The word of the LORD you have spoken is good," Hezekiah replied. For he thought, "Will there not be peace and security in my lifetime?"*
>
> 2 Kings 20: 16-19 NIV

Whoa. The country of Judah was going to be conquered by an enemy. Hezekiah's own kids and grandkids would be dragged from the palace and made to serve a pagan king. Some would be made into eunuchs ... which is pretty nasty fate, right?

But did you catch Hezekiah's response? He didn't react at all the way he did when he was sick. He didn't pray earnestly. He didn't weep. He didn't plead with God for the future of his grandkids as he had for his own future. In fact, Hezekiah was relieved because the horrible things were going to happen to his grandkids ... not to himself. That's just a tiny bit hard to respect, wouldn't you agree?

Sadly, King Hezekiah's grandkids didn't have a prayer. Not from Grandpa Hezekiah, anyway. He was too self-absorbed. That doesn't have to be the situation with your grandkids, though.

"But I don't know how to pray for my grandkids. Their world is so ... different." We hear you. And that's what this book is for. This is a guide to lead you in how to pray for your grandkids ... who happen to live in a very dark and dangerous world. A world where an enemy wants to steal them away and make them serve him ... instead of them serving our Lord and Savior, Jesus Christ.

The stakes are high. And your prayers can make a difference ... because you'll be bringing your petitions for your grandkids to the throne of Almighty God—in the powerful name of Jesus.

"They don't have a prayer" is something that never needs to be said about your grandkids. Now they do have a prayer. A whole book of prayers, in fact. And you'll be the one praying for them.

What a terrific way to show your love for your grandkids, right? Enjoy the prayer journey, knowing you're doing something really, really important for those grandkids!

Tim Shoemaker is the author of the award-winning *Escape From the Everglades*, the first in the Focus on the Family series for grandkids 12 and up, and *The Very Best, Hands-On, Kinda Dangerous Family Devotions, 52 Activities Your Kids Will Never Forget*

How to Use this 40 Day Prayer Guide

Prayer pages:

The guide will give you one daily theme with requests to pray for your grandchild for 40 days. If something interrupts your schedule, pick up the next prayer when you can.

You can simply pray the prayer to yourself or out loud as it is, or you can let the Holy Spirit guide you and use your own words.

Or these prayers can be a springboard for your prayer time as the Holy Spirit brings more things to mind as you pray.

For instance, there may be times when a particular problem or situation will take precedence over a pre-planned agenda of prayer.

And there may be times when the Holy Spirit leads you to a different topic for blessing. Go for it.

Being flexible and sensitive to the Holy Spirit is the most important thing. Simply being intentional and consistent in your prayer time will help you be sensitive to the Holy Spirit.

Reflect, Show & Share Pages:

Every 7 days the Guide will give you opportunities to:

- Write down what God is showing you about Himself, your grandchild, or yourself as you go along.
- Find ways to interact with your grandchild through conversations or activities.
- Consider your own memories of your grandparents, and how they impacted your life.
- See how He is speaking to you personally about your prayer life, or how God might be leading you in your life.

Appendix Resources

Check out our Appendix at the back of this book for valuable resources you might need during your 40 Day Journey or after. We've got prayers you can pray as your grandchild passes through different stages.

Whether it's how to put on spiritual armor before praying or checking out a list of ideas for conversations or activities with your grandchild, we've got you covered.

Before Beginning

Are you willing to set aside a few minutes each day to pray? We hope to encourage you and accompany you on your 40 day journey with day by day prayers. We also understand that sometimes things get in the way that are unavoidable. If you have to miss a day, simply pick up where you left off. You don't want to miss out on a blessing or hearing from God.

It may help to find a specific place or regular time of day to be sure you are being intentional and consistent in your praying (like when you first get up, or while exercising, on your way to work or during a break from work, or in a room or seat in your home at a certain time, or at a natural break in your daily routine).

In preparing for prayer, two areas are important:"

1. **Confession and Repentance** - The Bible tells us in Psalm 66:18 "If I had cherished sin in my heart, the Lord would not have listened." So it is important to take time to ask God to search your heart and show you any sin you need to confess and repent of before you move into interceding for someone.

God has promised that "If we confess our sins, He is faithful and just and will forgive us our sins and purify us from all unrighteousness." (1 John 1:9)

2. **Spiritual Armor for Battle** - Paul tells us to be "Strong in the Lord and in His mighty power. Put on the full armor of God." (Ephesians 6:10-11). So we need to do that—name and pray on each piece before we pray for others.

There are, of course, many things you can pray in asking God to strengthen, protect, and guide your grandchild. This is not meant to list or speak to all of them.

It is, however, my hope to help you be more intentional and consistent in praying. And by spending time in prayer, you will be open to the Spirit's leading. Learning to listen to the Holy Spirit guide you is most important.

It is my desire to help you grow in your prayer life as you pray. That you and your grandchild will benefit from the answers to your prayers. And that you will be blessed as you *Lean in and Learn from the Lord* through prayer.

Prayer tips

Are all prayers equal? It seems that God has listed some guidelines for us in Scripture that can either compromise or boost the effectiveness of our prayers.

There are even things that can cause Him to choose to step back or even disregard our prayers for a time. Yikes! Others are just the opposite, creating a multiplying effect on our prayers.

Have a look through and make sure nothing listed is going to get in your way over the next 40 days.

Some Biblical Guidelines

- "The prayer of a righteous person is powerful and effective" (James 5:16).

  Be sure you're following God and steering away from anything unrighteous or purposefully against God's ways for living. Holding grudges, being angry, indulging in wrongful thoughts or actions can all take away from the effectiveness of your 40 day journey.
- "The eyes of the Lord are on the righteous, and his ears are attentive to their cry" (Psalm 34:15).

  Exactly the opposite, we can rest assured we have God's complete attention when pursuing right living in our actions and choices.
- "Then Jesus told his disciples a parable to show them that they should always pray and not give up" (Luke 18:1).

  No worries there, you're going to be praying for the next 40 days, so you've got this!
- "When you ask you do not receive, because you ask with wrong motives, that you may spend what you get on your pleasures" (James 4:3).

  Okay, so praying for your boss to be blessed just so you get a promotion is not allowed, agreed?
- "But your iniquities have separated you from your God; your sins have hidden his face from you, so that he will not hear" (Isaiah 59:2).

  Again, let's be careful we don't have sin in our hearts that will get in the way of what we're asking. If we want to see the stars, let's get away from light pollution. If we want to talk to God, let's clear out the background noise and use a strong signal with four bars.
- "This is the confidence we have in approaching God: that if we ask anything according to his will, he hears us" (1 John 5:14).

Let's all be sure we're asking for things in line with His will, His plans, His timing, and not our own. Trust that God is actively working to draw this person to Him, and bless them for His Glory, even if we're not seeing anything happening right away.

Additional ideas that can boost the impact of your praying

- Pray these prayers out loud
  Does it help God hear them better? No. Does it help you? You bet! Praying out loud helps you slow down and focus on the person and words you're praying - allowing time for the Holy Spirit to meet you in your prayer. And that can make a difference all on its own.

- As the Holy Spirit brings additional things to mind when you're praying, pray those too
  The Holy Spirit knows best what this person needs and what will bless them.

- Pray the daily prayer multiple times a day
  When you eat. Morning and Evening. Or maybe whenever you start your car. When you think of the person you're praying for.

- Pray for more than one person
  What happens if you say two people's names for each prayer?

- Pray this 40 Day journey with a friend,
  Both of you, lifting up the same person in prayer. Or each of you praying for your own someone but checking in with each other on your journeys.

- Consider fasting at some point during the journey
  Giving up TV, social media, or even certain foods for a week during your journey will only serve to sharpen your spiritual focus!

Table of Contents

Dear Jesus

Dear Jesus keep these children in Your loving care
Be their Guide and Comfort when I can't be there
Teach them to obey You and to do what's right
Bless these sleeping children, bless them day and night

Thank You for the privilege of watching how they sleep
Though You let them come through me, they're not mine to keep
You have let me love them with all of my heart
Yet I know a time will come when we'll have to part

So Jesus keep these children in Your loving care
Be their Guide and Comfort when I can't be there
Teach them to obey You and to do what's right
Bless these sleeping children, Jesus, bless the children
Bless these sleeping children, bless them day and night

DAY 1

My Commitment

Proverbs 17:6, ***Children's children are a crown to the aged, and parents are the pride of their children.***

Heavenly Father, in the power of the name of the Lord Jesus Christ, I am offering these prayers. I am trusting You to act and effect Your will during these next 40 days of prayer for my grandchild _____, their life and our relationship. Pour out Your blessing on them whatever stage of life they are in.

Father, first and foremost, _____ is Yours! Your creation. Your child. Guard and guide _____. Protect and direct their life. Overcome and defeat any and all evil or worldly influences in their life. Meet whatever needs they have physically, emotionally, relationally, medically, mentally, psychologically, and spiritually. If there is illness or injury, heal them. If there are wounds, restore _____ to full health.

If they have believed lies, bring them Your truth. If they are going the wrong way, get their attention and redirect them. Put them on the path of eternal life with You.

Help me be a godly influence in _____'s life. I pray that I will be a godly example to lead them and love them. Remind me to consider my words and actions in light of being that example to my grandchild. Be at work in all areas of my life, my grandchild's life and in our relationship.

As for me, I will put on Your spiritual armor every day for these 40 days. (Ephesians 6:10-17) I will intercede for _____, asking that You bless them and will *contend with those who contend with them and fight against those who fight against them* giving them victory over the enemies of their soul. (Psalm 35:1)

Father, please help me in my commitment to pray daily. I give this 40 day journey to You. Lead me and teach me as I intercede for _____. I humbly ask for Your will to be done in and through _____'s life. Open up the storehouse of blessing, and let Your love and blessing pour over them to show them that You care, always. Amen

DAY 2

Relationship with You

John 3:16, ***For God so loved the world that he gave his one and only Son, that whoever believes in him shall not perish but have eternal life.***

Heavenly Father, You know best what they need and how to help them find their way to You. Only You call. And only You save.

I pray that from an early age, _____ will have an awareness of You. Give them a spiritual discernment to sense who You are as their Heavenly Father, their Creator, and the One who loves them and will never leave them.

Whether it's from songs they learn, like Jesus Loves Me, or Bible stories, or being taken to church, being prayed over personally, or from the way You choose to communicate with them…give my grandchild a real understanding of Your love for them. An unconditional love, a sacrificial love, greater than any other they will ever know.

And at the appropriate time, teach _____ about the problem of sin. And how although it separates us from You, You made a way: Jesus lived a sinless life and shed His blood on the cross to pay the price our sin demanded. Help them understand that His blood is the free gift that pays the penalty for their sin, once and for all. And that accepting that gift allows _____ to be in relationship with You for all eternity.

Remove the blinders if _____ has believed lies keeping them in darkness. Reward even the tiniest baby steps they take in Your direction. Help _____ surrender whatever they need to lay aside to be in close fellowship with You. Help them tear down the walls they have constructed that keep them away from You. And in Your might and power, tear down any strongholds the evil one has built in their life.

Lead _____ to walk in the freedom of Your relationship with them. Let _____ know they can come to You with any joy, any sadness, any problem, and that You are there for them to help, to heal and to encourage them their whole life. That there is no problem too big or too small for You to handle. Amen

DAY 3

Our Relationship

Ecclesiastes 4:9-10, ***Two are better than one, because they have a good return for their labor: if either of them falls down, one can help the other up. But pity anyone who falls and has no one to help them up.***

Heavenly Father, please keep my relationship with my grandchild, _____, a priority for me. Thank You for this precious family member. Let ours be a relationship that glorifies You and benefits and encourages us both.

Let me show Your love to _____ in the ways I speak to and act toward them. Guard my words and actions so I can teach them to love and worship You not only in words, but in how I behave and live. Help me protect _____ and be a resource they can come to in need. Show me how to build them up and help them live a godly life in whatever stage they are in.

I want to share in the joys and sorrows, and all the regular days in between, in _____'s life. Teach me what I need to know to support, cry with and celebrate with my grandchild. Show me when to speak and when to be silent, when to act and when to just listen.

Thank You Father, for whatever time I have to be in _____'s life. Let there be open and honest communication between us. I pray there will be times when we work together toward a goal, whether learning something new or managing some task. And also times when we can simply relax and enjoy each other's company.

Father, let my grandchild _____ grow in wisdom, in stature and in favor with You and man. Amen

DAY 4

Family

2 Corinthians 13:11, ***Strive for full restoration, encourage one another, be of one mind, live in peace. And the God of love and peace will be with you.***

Heavenly Father, help _____ relate well to their immediate family: parents, brothers and sisters, grandparents, aunts and uncles. I ask for Your blessing over this family. Protect them from tragedy and trauma. Draw each one of them to know You as Savior, to worship You as a family, and to turn to You with problems. Teach them to seek Your wisdom in making plans and living their lives.

Encourage open and honest communication among all family members, allowing each one to be able to be honest about their physical, emotional and spiritual needs. Meet whatever needs _____ has in dealing with family members. Encourage them all to speak the truth in love. (Ephesians 4:15)

Lead _____'s family to a Bible teaching church where they can hear and study Your word and worship in a community of Believers. Where they can discover their spiritual gifts and use those. Where they can find the support and encouragement they need to raise their family to know and worship You and live by godly values.

When difficulties arise, give special wisdom to _____'s parents as they make decisions that affect the entire family regarding their marriage, parenting, work, money, home management, relocations, travel. If the difficulties are relational, provide bridge-building opportunities for the members to work things out bringing restoration and unity.

Make _____'s family a source of joy and strength and support in their life.

Father, let my grandchild _____ grow in wisdom, in stature and in favor with You and man. Amen

DAY 5

Friends

Proverbs 12:26, ***The righteous choose their friends carefully, but the way of the wicked leads them astray.***

Heavenly Father, I pray for the relationships with friends my grandchild ____ will have throughout their lifetime. Bring people alongside them who will be good friends. Let them be like iron sharpening iron, not iron poking iron, keeping each other accountable and pointed in a godly direction. Help _____ choose their friends wisely, understanding that bad company corrupts good character. (1 Corinthians 15:33).

Father, bring friends into _____'s life at all stages who are kind and caring—

- as a growing child, bring friends to play with and learn about sharing and communicating.
- in school, bring someone to learn with, sit with at lunchtime, play on the playground with.
- as a teen, bring trustworthy friends who will be accountable, give godly advice, keep confidences, and be a godly influence.
- as a young adult, bring people who love You and make wise decisions, listening to Your voice over the temptations of the world and the flesh.

Father, help _____ not "judge a book by its cover" but get to know the person regardless of outward differences. Produce in _____ godly character traits of being a good friend like honesty, loyalty, kindness, caring, and generosity. Let them gain and give help, support, encouragement, and accountability to know and do the right thing.

Father, let my grandchild _____ grow in wisdom, in stature and in favor with You and man. Amen

DAY 6

Identity

Psalm 139:14, ***I praise you because I am fearfully and wonderfully made; your works are wonderful. I know that full well.***

Heavenly Father, give my grandchild _____ an awareness and an appreciation of the unique way You have created them. Thank You for giving _____ the positive traits that I see in them, and others that will develop in time. Help them see themself through Your

eyes, from Your perspective, and let that be the source of their sense of true value and worth.

Help my grandchild understand the special personality, abilities, and experiences that affect who they are today, and show them how those gifts will benefit them in the future. Teach _____ that their actions do not determine their identity, but that the identity You give them as a child of God—determines their actions.

Do not allow _____ to define who they are or their worth by the social values of the world. Show _____ that they are more than their reflection in the mirror. Give them a healthy body image however they look. Even if they don't care for some physical attribute, help them understand their worth is not based on their worst feature, but on the person inside.

And don't let _____ be defined by the grades they get or their performance in activities. Draw them to recreation, hobbies and interests that are based on skills and abilities that they have—something they're good at. And whether it's an area of schoolwork, sports, music, or art, help them work for their best personal or team effort. Provide support to help them work on and improve their skill.

If that means winning, let them be an example of winning happily, but humbly. If it means losing or failing, show them how to lose gracefully, learn what they can, and move forward. All too often our sense of worth suffers if we don't meet someone else's expected level of performance. But You, Father, love _____ regardless of what they do or how well they do it. You love _____ because of who they are.

Show _____ the great value they have because they are Your child, Your creation, Your beloved son or daughter. Help me remind them how much I love them and of Your love for them.

Remind them of these truths through the Bible. Scripture reveals:

_____ *is chosen by You, holy and dearly loved,*
_____ *is Your child,*
_____ *is Your workmanship,*
_____ *is fearfully and wonderfully made,*
_____ *is free forever from condemnation,*
_____ is the beloved whom You *rejoice over with singing!*

Father, let my grandchild _____ grow in wisdom, in stature and in favor with You and man. Amen

DAY 7

Spiritual Protection

Ephesians 6:12, ***For our struggle is not against flesh and blood, but against the rulers, against the authorities, against the powers of this dark world and against the spiritual forces of evil in the heavenly realms.***

Heavenly Father, protect and guide my grandchild _____'s comings and goings. Do not let _____ seek after evil or be tempted by the temporary pleasures of evil. Help them see evil for what it is.

You tell us there are spiritual enemies who seek to undermine my grandchild's faith and ability to do the work You created them to do. So I put _____'s name into Psalm 35 and pray Your words against every ruler, authority and power of this dark world, and the spiritual forces in the heavenly realms who set themselves against You and Your will for _____, in order to protect their life, health, family, relationships, home, school, work, finances, mental and emotional well-being and spiritual growth.

Psalm 35 Of David.

Contend, Lord, with those who contend with _____; fight against those who fight against _____.

Take up shield and armor; arise and come to their *aid.*

Brandish spear and javelin against those who pursue _____.

Say to _____, "I am your salvation."

May those who seek _____'s life be disgraced and put to shame; may those who plot their ruin be turned back in dismay.

May they be like chaff before the wind, with the angel of the Lord driving them away; may their path be dark and slippery, with the angel of the Lord pursuing them.

Since they hid their net for _____ without cause and without cause dug a pit for _____, may ruin overtake them by surprise—may the net they hid entangle them, may they fall into the pit, to their ruin.

Then my soul will rejoice in the Lord and delight in his salvation.

My whole being will exclaim, "Who is like you, Lord?

Then she scratched her nose.
And when she put her hand back down, it was on the
tween them, her little finger brushing against the outside of his
thigh. He felt it, and she left it there. Another twenty minutes
by, another twenty minutes of effortless, breathy talk, none of it

How long, Lord, will you look on? Rescue _____ from their ravages, their precious life from these lions.

I will give you thanks in the great assembly; among the throngs I will praise you.

Do not let those gloat over _____ who are their enemies without cause; do not let those who hate _____ without reason maliciously wink the eye.

They do not speak peaceably, but devise false accusations against those who live quietly in the land.

They sneer at _____ and say, "Aha! Aha! With our own eyes we have seen it."

Lord, you have seen this; do not be silent. Do not be far from _____, Lord.

Awake, and rise to _____'s defense! Contend for them, my God and Lord.

Vindicate _____ in your righteousness, Lord my God; do not let them gloat over _____.

Do not let them think, "Aha, just what we wanted!" or say, "We have swallowed them up."

May all who gloat over _____'s distress be put to shame and confusion; may all who exalt themselves over _____ be clothed with shame and disgrace.

May those who delight in _____'s vindication shout for joy and gladness; may they always say, "The Lord be exalted, who delights in the well-being of his servant."

My tongue will proclaim Your righteousness, Your praises all day long.

Father, let my grandchild _____ grow in wisdom, in stature and in favor with You and man. Amen

Reflect, Show & Share

How are you doing so far? If you have been able to be consistent in praying this week—good for you!
If not, what has gotten in your way?

How can you remedy that?

If you missed any prayers, just pick up tomorrow where you left off. During your prayer time has God shown you anything new about Himself? About your grandchild, or about yourself?

♥ In person, on Zoom, Facetime, or through the mail, consider showing _____photos of yourself and your family, and of your grandchild. Use current photos, and if you have them, photos of when you or their parents were their age.

♥ Share the story of what was happening when the picture was taken, where you were, what was important to you then, and what the world was like then.

→Have new pictures taken or videos made of you and your grandchild together. Consider putting them into an album, notebook or place on your phone you can look at them together often. Or text with them to say—"Hey, I was thinking about when we did (whatever is in the photo) and wanted to say Hi!"

♥ Show them something you have from a family trip, vacation or adventure. Or give them something you brought for them from a place or trip you went on. And share that story

♥ Show them something that reminds you of a friend of yours, and tell them what you like about that friend.

→Ask if they have a friend, what they like about that friend and what kind of things they do together.

Your ideas to Reflect, Show or Share

My mother told me a study was done at two elementary schools: one in the community and one on a nearby military base. The children were asked to draw their grandparents.

The community school children drew happy, smiling grandparents. The military base school children drew more pictures with the grandparents crying.

My dad was in the military so I usually went to schools on base. We tried to see my grandparents with every transfer, but it didn't always work out. And we were in France for three years and didn't see them at all. So we would show up in Texas, on our way to Arizona, Kansas, New Jersey, Virginia, or France and stay for a few days. And when we'd leave, they would stand there, waving and crying. Knowing they wouldn't see us for another whole year, or more. So I get the pictures of crying.

But we made the most of our time together! I have amazing memories at all ages, of spending wonderful times with my grandparents—they played games with me, taught me how to do things, let me help them with chores, cooking, work on the car—even if I just sat behind the wheel while granddaddy replaced parts and talked to me.

I LOVED spending time with them. They always made time for me, and I felt completely loved.

Whatever time you have—YOU can make a difference in your grandchild's life.

DAY 8

Sleep

Psalm 4:8, ***In peace I will lie down and sleep, for You alone, Lord, make me dwell in safety.***

Heavenly Father, even from an early age, send my grandchild _____ safe, sweet sleep that comes quickly and easily. Let _____'s sleep be regenerative: providing rest, energy, and healing for their body and peaceful restoration for their soul. No matter the kind of day they had, provide sleep at night that will help their mind function well: to manage and organize the thoughts of the previous day and sort out new information, cataloging it into memory.

As a baby and child, _____ will need adequate sleep that keeps their body and mind growing. In school they will need to sleep so they awake ready to focus with mental clarity on the day's learning. And as _____ processes relationships and life around them, help them learn to let go of random and worrying thoughts and the stresses of the day to fall asleep and sleep soundly through the night.

Father, at every age, protect _____ from nightmares and fears that cause emotional turmoil at bedtime. When _____ is tired, don't let them fight it. Help them listen to their body to get the sleep they need. Show _____ how to recognize the signals her body gives: fuzzy thinking, inability to focus attention, irritability, silliness.

Since sleep needs change with age, stress, health, and other factors, don't let _____ work to the point of physical or mental exhaustion. As they begin to set their own sleep schedule, give _____ wisdom and discernment to prioritize sleep. Bless _____ by letting them wake up feeling ready to face each day, energized, able to focus on all that lies ahead; feeling physically rested, mentally alert, emotionally clear, and spiritually at peace.

Father, let my grandchild _____ grow in wisdom, in stature and in favor with You and man. Amen

DAY 9

Changes

Philippians 4:6-7, ***Do not be anxious about anything, but in every situation, by prayer and petition, with thanksgiving, present your requests to God. And the peace of God, which transcends all understanding, will guard your hearts and your minds in Christ Jesus.***

Heavenly Father, life is made up of change. As my grandchild _____ grows and matures, change will come inwardly to their body, mind, emotions, hormones and more. Outwardly, _____ may move to different places or change schools, friends, social groups, jobs.

Help my grandchild embrace all these changes in a positive way. And recognize ways You are building into them or providing what they will need, resources that will help them handle these changes. Keeping the child-like innocence and wonder alive all their lives.

As _____ learns and grows help them understand their body and the normal changes that signal maturity in a positive way. Help them accept their maturity and lay aside childish things and ways. Growth can bring new privileges and responsibilities. Bring support alongside _____ to help them understand the changes and make the most of the opportunities their maturity brings.

Moving to a new place brings the challenges of saying goodbye to people, places and activities, but also brings the possibilities and joy of meeting new people and making new friends. Going to a new school or getting a new brother or sister may mean sharing becomes a way of life, but expands their ability to love someone new and have a new partner in the family to love and share with, learn from and play with. Help _____ see, accept, and rejoice in the positive side of changes in their life.

Father, bring someone into _____'s life who will help them see the positives, show them how to adapt, and make the most of the situation. Teach _____ to call on You, understanding there is no problem too big or too small for You to help them with.

Father, let my grandchild _____ grow in wisdom, in stature and in favor with You and man. Amen

DAY 10

Laughter

Job 8:21, ***He will yet fill your mouth with laughter and your lips with shouts of joy.***

Heavenly Father, bring joy and laughter to my grandchild, _____. Every day let them see something that makes them smile. Your Word tells us that laughter is good medicine for the soul. And a happy heart brings life to the bones. (Proverbs 17:22)

Father gift my grandchild with a good sense of humor and wonder at the world. Let being outside playing or taking a walk or seeing Your Creation through a window or in a picture put a smile on their face. Let _____ find joy in watching tiny ants or grasshoppers, or seeing shapes in the clouds. As they grow, give them a continued sense of amazement at the world You've created for them to live in.

When stressful things occur, don't allow the negative to overtake _____'s focus or cloud their mind. A good sense of humor can lessen my grandchild's burden, whatever the need. Rekindle their sense of humor to lighten the load. Let laughter be a balm for their soul.

Bring people into _____'s life who make them smile and laugh and encourage _____ to spend time with them. Whether taking a break to call a friend and tell a joke, watch a funny cartoon or movie, read a comic book, or just a fun break from work, show _____ where they can set aside time to drop the seriousness of life and literally laugh out loud. And let that energize them for the tasks before them.

What did the man say when all his lamps were stolen? I'm delighted!

Father, let my grandchild _____ grow in wisdom, in stature and in favor with You and man. Amen

DAY 11

Pride vs Humility

Philippians 2:3-4, ***Do nothing out of selfish ambition or vain conceit. Rather, in humility value others above yourselves, not looking to your own interests but each of you to the interests of the others.***

Heavenly Father, do not let my grandchild _____ walk in prideful conceit or arrogance. Do not allow them to think of themselves as more worthy or valuable than other people.

I thank You for making _____ so unique and special in accordance with Your perfect plan for them. Let _____ see their value as Your child, created individually by You. But not in a way that puts other people down, or elevates them to feeling more important than others.

Father, help _____ be good at things and worthy of respect and admiration, but without a prideful attitude. Teach _____ to turn away from selfish ambition, vanity, conceitedness and any attitude of superiority. Instead, in serving others, let _____ look to others' needs and submit to the authorities You have placed in their life.

You tell us that pride goes before a fall (Proverbs 16:8) and that we should humble ourselves (James 4:10) and leave the lifting up to You. Show _____ how to treat everyone with respect as Your beloved children. Teach _____ not to judge themselves or people by outward appearances, but to look inward to character.

When _____ makes a mistake, prompt them to respond with humility, and if necessary, ask forgiveness and make amends. And in victory, show _____ how to celebrate humbly, giving rightful praise and honor to You.

Father, let my grandchild _____ grow in wisdom, in stature and in favor with You and man. Amen

DAY 12

Mentors and Role Models

2 Timothy 3:14, ***...continue in what you have learned and have become convinced of, because you know those from whom you learned it.***

Heavenly Father, please bring spiritual mentors and role models into my grandchild _____'s life. Let their mentor be someone who is spiritually mature and can counsel and support them from a position of godly wisdom and experience. You know the kind of person that can impact and influence _____. Send someone they will respect and listen to who will make an impression on them at every age.

Provide opportunities for mentors to take an active interest in _____'s life; and to observe and speak into all kinds of issues and situations. And give these mentors Your wisdom to know how to interact with and be involved with _____ in a natural, relaxed way.

Father, provide godly role models who will speak the truth and show _____ how to live a godly life in this ungodly world. Let these people demonstrate how to make wise decisions. Let their behavior speak into _____'s life of how to live out godly values even if others around them are not.

Whether in the family, in church, at school, in the community, or in the world, let _____ see and imitate people who live with integrity, honesty, kindness, courage, and self-control.

Thank You for the way You use ordinary people in our lives for extraordinary purposes.

Father, let my grandchild _____ grow in wisdom, in stature and in favor with You and man. Amen

DAY 13

Screens

Proverbs 25:28, ***Like a city whose walls are broken through is a person who lacks self-control.***

Colossians 3:1, ***...set your hearts on things above, where Christ is, seated at the right hand of God. Set your minds on things above, not on earthly things.***

Heavenly Father, from a young age, do not let my grandchild _____ become overly attached to screens. There are so many opportunities these days to become dependent on screens and even prefer them to personal contact.

Television, video games of all kinds, tablets with puzzles, social media and games, phones used for texting and getting drawn into hours of scanning information and misinformation, and computers, can all become an escape from personal interaction with our loved ones. It can become an obsession, or even an addiction.

Give _____ a healthy interest in enjoying time outside, in the three-Dimensional world. And being around people of all kinds, to play with, learn from and share with. Let there be undirected time for them to marvel at the beauty of the world, look at the sky and the clouds, watch insects, grow flowers and vegetables, play with a pet, be creative with music or art or mud pies.

Let _____ respect limits their parents set for screen time to prevent sleep disturbances, neck and back problems, vision issues, decreased creativity, and weight gain with eating troubles. Give my grandchild a love of You and Your world outside. Draw their interest to spending time in the real world, learning and listening, playing and exploring and connecting with You, the Creator.

Help _____'s parents, and even me, model healthy behavior in this way also. Let me demonstrate that spending time in person with them is more important to me than my own screens.

Father, let my grandchild _____ grow in wisdom, in stature and in favor with You and man. Amen

DAY 14

Making Mistakes

Psalm 103:13-14, ***As a father has compassion on his children, so the Lord* has compassion on those who fear him; *for he knows how we are formed, he remembers that we are dust.***

Heavenly Father, I praise You that You are a God of second chances...and third...and fourth. Please encourage my grandchild _____ that they are not judged by their greatest shame or mistake.

Thank You that You know _____'s weaknesses and strengths. And that when they err, You provide grace and the opportunity to learn to trust You more. Teach my grandchild to come to You in humility when in the wrong, but to also know that Your forgiveness is complete and Your grace is sufficient for them.

So much of growing up is by trial and error. As they grow, show _____ how to learn from their mistakes so they won't make the same ones again. And as they see others make mistakes, let them learn without having to make those mistakes themselves.

Place people around _____ who will help coach and teach them, and show by example, how to make the most of their opportunities. And when mistakes are made, how to cope with failure and move forward.

Protect _____ from being trapped by guilt and shame, but to make apologies or amends to others where needed. And to come to You humbly seeking forgiveness and direction when necessary.

Father, let my grandchild _____ grow in wisdom, in stature and in favor with You and man. Amen

Reflect, Show & Share

Second week—how's it going? If you have been able to be consistent in praying this week—way to go!
If not, what has gotten in your way?

How can you remedy that?

If you missed any prayers, just pick up tomorrow where you left off. During your prayer time has God shown you anything new about Himself? About your grandchild, or about yourself?

♥ Show your grandchild a book and read it to them about going to sleep, or a bedtime story. If you can, ask to put them to bed at bedtime. Share different places you've slept: in a car, train, boat, tent, airport, bus, bunk bed, sleeping bag, on the floor

♥ Ask what they do when they can't fall asleep and share things that have helped you, or haven't. If appropriate, share a good night prayer.

→Tell a joke, make silly faces, make a funny noise, pretend to fall down to make your grandchild laugh. Have a tickle fest with each other. Then tell them not to laugh and see who laughs first

♥ Share about big changes in your life growing up and how you coped with those. Ask about any approaching changes in their life and point out positive aspects and benefits of the changes, and how to make the most of the down sides

→Look deep into their eyes and tell them something you love about them

→Take a short walk and talk about what you see, hear, smell or can pick up like rocks or leaves to remember the walk

→Go outside and watch the sky: clouds—what they look like, a storm in the distance with lightening, sunset, sunrise,

- ♥ Share who you wanted to be like when you grew up and why. Ask who they want to be like, and why
- ♥ Share a mistake you made one time and what you learned from it, or a mistake someone else you know made and what you learned from it.

Your ideas to Reflect, Show or Share

____

____

____

____

____

When I was just able to walk, my grandmother Minnie and I would spend time every evening watering her flower beds. She would let me hold the hose and direct the water. I dragged the hose from one bed to another and watched the brown dirt around the plants turn a deep rich black with moisture, then make little rivers from one plant to the next.

I even liked it when the water splashed on the concrete sidewalk, making a darkened trail where you could follow my movements from one place to another. Or when we walked through it and made visible footprints.

So many things I do on a daily basis are not like that at all. They don't give me that sense of satisfaction of being able to literally see where I've been and how I've made a difference.

I think that's why I love to work in the yard and garden. When I've weeded or planted, I can see a difference in where I've been. It makes me feel like I've accomplished something. Like I've made a difference. And it all goes back to the early memories and home movies of me and my grandmother, watering the flowers.

DAY 15

Love for the Bible

John 17:17, (Jesus prays) ***Sanctify them by the truth, your word is truth.***

John 8:32, ***Then you will know the truth and the truth will set you free.***

Heavenly Father, let my grandchild _____ hear stories in the Bible from a young age. At every age, open their mind and spirit to the truth found there. Establish in their understanding that the Bible is more than just another book; that it teaches about You, The Creator of the world and all things in it, including them. And that it teaches about Your love, Your faithfulness, and that You are true to all Your promises.

As _____ grows, teach them to read Your Word, all of scripture, with an openness to what it's saying to them personally, specifically, so they gain strength and understanding from it. Show them how to put their name into scripture to personalize the meaning and read it out loud. Here's an example:

> "I, _____ will not fear for You, Lord, are with me; I will not be dismayed for You are my God. You will strengthen me, _____ and help me, You will uphold me, _____ with Your righteous right hand." (Isaiah 41:10)

Draw _____ to Yourself through Your Word. Let them grow to love The Bible and learn valuable lessons from the characters and circumstances. Let it light their path in the world, leading them and protecting them. Heavenly Father, let Your Word be implanted into good soil in _____. And reap a harvest of victory in their salvation!

When they read or hear or even memorize Your Word, let it stick with them even into adulthood. So they can recall, and call on Your Word when they need wisdom. As Your word is read and taught to them let it not return void, but produce in and accomplish through _____ all You desire in their life. (Isaiah 55:11)

Father, let my grandchild _____ grow in wisdom, in stature and in favor with You and man. Amen

DAY 16

Sense Your Presence

Psalm 16:11, ***You make known to me the path of life; you will fill me with joy in your presence, with eternal pleasures at your right hand.***

Heavenly Father, I pray that You would help my grandchild _____ sense Your presence from a young age. Let them somehow know that You are their Heavenly Father. That You created them. That You love them. That You will protect them. And that You have good plans for their life.

Let them hear scriptures and stories from the Bible. Teach them songs that speak of Your love for them even as little children. And let that sense of Your presence with them grow as they grow. Let _____ feel You with them in real and tangible ways—an answered prayer, help when they need it, an unexpected blessing.

Do not let _____ be misled by believing things that happen to them are just luck, or karma or some mystical power of the universe or powerful person. As they search, draw _____ to Yourself, and protect them from any other power that might seek to do them harm.

May Your constant presence give my grandchild a sense of calm and peace on a daily basis. And bring an awesome reassurance of security that _____ can feel, even through challenging circumstances and difficult situations.

Father, let my grandchild _____ grow in wisdom, in stature and in favor with You and man. Amen

DAY 17

Hear Your Voice

Psalm 95:7, ***for he is our God and we are the people of his pasture, the flock under his care. Today, if only you would hear his voice***

Heavenly Father, give my grandchild _____ the experience of knowing that You are speaking to them personally. Show them how to recognize Your voice and what You are saying to them. And how You guide them in and through the circumstances of their life.

You may not speak to them audibly, but in whatever way You choose to reach out and communicate with them, teach _____ how to discern Your voice from all the other voices they hear—those from the world, those in their own mind, and those from the evil one. Like sheep know the voice of their Shepherd let _____ become familiar with the sound of Your voice and be responsive to what You have to say to them.

As _____ grows, open their spiritual ears to hear all You would say. Let them hear first of all about Your amazing, unconditional love for them. About how You created them uniquely, and accept them the way they are. Speak to _____ about Your caring and Your protection. And when they are older, regarding their life purpose, their circumstances, their relationships, business and personal decisions.

Just like a radio receiver has to be tuned in to the right frequency to hear the station broadcasting, teach _____ how to "tune" their spirit to hear You speak: be it from the Bible, in prayer, from sermons or podcasts, from other people, by observing nature, through their circumstances, in dreams or visions, or through joys or even pain.

Let _____ know when they hear from You that it is indeed You, and how to confirm that. Make it clear how You are leading them. You have given _____ ears to hear, let them hear. (Mark 4:9)

Father, let my grandchild _____ grow in wisdom, in stature and in favor with You and man. Amen

DAY 18

Strong Faith

Colossians 4:12, ***...stand firm in all the will of God, mature and fully assured.***

Heavenly Father, I pray that my grandchild _____ would make their faith their own and grow strong in that faith. From an early age, allow _____ to sense Your presence with them, protecting and directing them. As they turn to You, meet their needs in tangible ways they will understand is Your hand at work in their life.

Bring teachers who will be able to articulate to a child what having faith means. Grant _____ a mature understanding of the meaning of scripture and how it applies to their life. Help them learn how to live out what the Bible teaches in their words and actions, being not just a hearer or the Word but a doer also. (James 1:22)

Teach _____ to know why they believe what they believe. And let that knowledge be the strength they need to keep them from giving in to temptation. Let that knowledge empower them to live their life courageously; encouraging others along the way, and persevering in difficulty.

Continue to deepen _____'s faith throughout their life. Help them live trusting in You with hope for their future. Bring whatever they need in the circumstances they're dealing with. Even when things don't look good from an earthly perspective, let _____ look to Your promises and to You as Way Maker and Promise Keeper who will never leave them.

Father, let my grandchild _____ grow in wisdom, in stature and in favor with You and man. Amen

DAY 19

Drugs and Ungodly Influences

I Peter 5:8, ***Your enemy the devil prowls around like a roaring lion looking for someone to devour.***

Heavenly Father, protect my grandchild _____ from ungodly influences in the world. Advertising and social media spew a worldview of selfishness and greed, and worse, have become a platform for supporting terrorism, sex, drugs, abuse and death. What can seem harmless to an adult can be sensational and inviting to a child. And it comes 24/7 if not supervised by a responsible adult.

Teachers, Coaches and friends become so important for the school age child. Parents are no longer the main source of information as children look to others. Protect _____ from any who would mislead or sway them to embrace a worldview based on the values of the world or take part in behaviors that would harm them. Protect them from evil teachings that lead away from godly values…from classes taught in school to lessons caught in sports, theater, music or other activities.

So many things are accepted and taught in the schools now that are contrary to what the Bible teaches. Younger students are exposed to different views of right and wrong. And older ones are taught social values on politics, lifestyles, identity, and sexuality. Protect _____ from the warped views that others lead or teach from. Do not allow those values to find a place in _____'s heart or get a foothold in their mind.

Teach _____ how drugs can destroy their life. That beyond the momentary "feel good" moments, lies unintended consequences and addiction. Let my grandchild learn from the mistakes others make to avoid terrible or even deadly consequences of being tempted into trying drugs. Do not let them believe the lies of drugs being harmless, or try and prove something, or fit in with others.

Strengthen _____'s faith and character from an early age to turn away from drugs and other ungodly influences.

Father, let my grandchild _____ grow in wisdom, in stature and in favor with You and man. Amen

DAY 20

Bullies

Luke 6:27-28, ***But to you who are listening I say: Love your enemies, do good to those who hate you, bless those who curse you, pray for those who mistreat you.***

Heavenly Father, protect my grandchild _____ from being bullied, and from becoming a bully. Give my grandchild the confidence and courage they need to stand up for themselves and others who need defending. Help them see beyond any physical threat and use their words and discernment to meet these challenges.

See to it that the adults in charge see and stop bullying, whether at school or in team or community/neighborhood activities. Call on people in positions of authority to enforce a "No Tolerance" attitude towards bullying. Strengthen and empower all students to report instances of bullying. And let the punishment be sufficient to stop bullying behavior.

Father, change the heart of the bully, deliver the bully from hateful and damaging behavior. And protect the target of this bad behavior from the harm that was intended.

Give _____ a heart for the outcast, the one who's always picked last, or the small child who can't defend themselves. Don't let _____ ever resort to behavior that would tease, demean, or humiliate others. Bring people my grandchild can go to when they or a friend is in need of help with bullying issues.

Father, You have the power to use everything for good so nothing is wasted. Use what was meant for evil here, for good. Do the same for bullies. Meet them where they are and transform their lives with Your love.

In the Bible, Paul persecuted Christians until he had an experience with You. And then he became a powerful spokesman and encourager for good. Lord, help all of us to be careful about writing off the bullies in our lives; you just never know.

Father, let my grandchild _____ grow in wisdom, in stature and in favor with You and man. Amen

DAY 21

Divine Appointments

Philippians 2:13, ***For it is God who works in you to will and to act in order to fulfill his good purpose.***

Heavenly Father, grant my grandchild _____ "Divine Appointments" throughout their life. Arrange opportunities for them to be in the right place at the right time to hear or see something or someone who will contribute to understanding Your love for _____ and Your provision and purpose for their life.

Orchestrate meetings with others who can introduce them to the answers they're looking for. Lead _____ to people who exemplify godly behavior, language and character and can be a blessing to them. And help them make the connection that You are providing for them.

Whether these will become lifelong friendships, or a momentary influence in _____'s life, let these happenings occur often. Create a constant stream of positive, godly and encouraging direction for _____.

Heavenly Father, You created the universe! Let _____ witness events or casual occurrences that make a connection with You and Your power. Help _____ discover You in a podcast or the theme of a movie or a real-life discussion. Let them see You in a joy or a challenge they experience. When these Divine Appointments happen, don't let _____ miss the significance of what is occurring. Open their mind and heart and spirit to the influences You bring their way.

Father, let my grandchild _____ grow in wisdom, in stature and in favor with You and man. Amen

Reflect, Show & Share

How are you doing so far? If you have been able to be consistent in praying this week—good for you!

If not, what has gotten in your way?

____

How can you remedy that?

____

____

If you missed any prayers, just pick up tomorrow where you left off.

During your prayer time has God shown you anything new about Himself? About your grandchild, or about yourself?

____

____

____

____

→Show them your Bible and read a verse or two to them that you like and share why you like it, what it means to you.

→Give them an age appropriate Bible (board book, picture book, easy reader, youth edition, Lego Bible!);

→Teach them a song to sing about Jesus: Jesus loves me, Jesus loves the little Children.

→Go to church with them or bring them to church with you.

→Watch a movie or video with them that teaches or shows godly values.

♥ Tell them about Jesus and your faith. Like where you went to church and what that was like.

♥ If there was a time you felt God working in your life, or leading you to a decision or in a direction, share what that felt like.

Your ideas to Reflect, Show or Share

My first funeral was my grandfather, Paw Paw. He had been sick with lung cancer so I saw him get sicker and weaker. It was the year we lived in my hometown while my dad was stationed in Korea, and he didn't make it home in time for his father's funeral.

The preacher knew our family and often came into my grandparents' store. He said HC was always showing him the products on the shelf that were "New and Improved." And that now he was in a "New and Improved" place in heaven. Where there was no more pain and no more suffering. I was happy for him since I had seen the pain and suffering on his face and heard it in his breathing.

Heaven became very real to me at that time. And I was resolved to not be afraid of dying, because I too, knew who Jesus was, and had asked Him to be my Lord of my life, and take me to be with Him in heaven. But I was never comfortable with what people often have to go through in life before they got there.

I didn't realize no one had told my father what the sermon was about until I repeated it at my grandmother MawMaw's funeral twenty years later. I wrote a song about it called ***New and Improved***. Seeing how my grandparents lived their lives and then pass on as they did gave me a certainty of my faith that there is more to come after this life.

Lyrics in the Appendix E

Halfway point check:

Have you sensed any pushback?

When you are praying intentionally and consistently, that does not make the evil one happy. You may sense pushback in finding yourself facing hardship or discouragement. Or there could be an upset with the grandchild you're praying for, or any other relationship, or your work or home life. Maybe a sudden health issue or unexplained crisis. It may seem to come out of the blue, with no warning and no logic as to why things are happening.

Have you experienced anything like that? What?

If this happens it could be spiritual, so it's helpful to be sure you are praying on the Armor of God as part of your daily prayer time. Even a simple prayer like:

Heavenly Father, thank You for the armor You give me that protects me as I pray. I put on the Helmet of Salvation to protect my mind, and the Breastplate of Righteousness as a protective cover for my heart. I put on the Belt of Truth to help me discern truth and reject any lies. I wear the Shoes of the Gospel of Peace and take up the Shield of Faith and the Sword of the Spirit to fight in the battles You call me to.

For more information see the Resource Guide on Spiritual Armor for Battle in the Appendix at the back of the book. Page #

And ask God to guard you and protect you, your family, your health, finances, relationships, home, job, and whatever else you feel led to pray about that could be attacked. Ask God to keep you standing firm.

It also helps to talk with another Christian friend and ask them to pray for you and what you're experiencing. Or even for the duration of this 40 day journey.

DAY 22

1st Commandment—Honor God

Exodus 20:3, ***You shall have no other gods before me.***

Proverbs 1:7, ***The fear of the Lord is the beginning of knowledge, but fools despise wisdom and instruction.***

Heavenly Father, I pray that my grandchild _____ will live a life of obedience to You. So I am praying they will learn, understand and obey Your Ten Commandments. Give _____ a true sense of awe and reverence for You, Your power, and Your love. Teach them who You are, how You created them, and how much You love them. Help _____ understand that You want to have a personal relationship with them, individually, and that you have a plan and purpose for their life.

Lord draw _____ to know You. Help them develop a "fear" of You, meaning a deep reverence and respect. Help them understand that only You are everywhere, all the time, with all power, knowing all things. And that even with the power of the universe, and holding the whole world in Your hands, You also bend down to hear their prayers and hold their precious face in those same, now gentle, hands.

Do not let my grandchild _____ put things like academics, sports, popularity, money, social activities, boy/girl or friend relationships, self, or any other thing before You in importance. Do not let them be led astray to worship any false god, person, power, creature, belief, religion, or philosophy. And let me model this in my life as I set priorities and spend my time. Let _____ see me honor You with my time, my money, my gifts. Let my life clearly show that You are my Number One priority.

I pray that You will help _____ learn how to balance their life, putting You first. Show them how to value and honor family, school, others, even our country, but to always place You first in priority.

Father, let my grandchild _____ grow in wisdom, in stature and in favor with You and man. Amen

DAY 23

No Idols

Exodus 20:4, ***You shall not make for yourself an image in the form of anything in heaven above or on the earth beneath or in the waters below. You shall not bow down to them or worship them.***

Heavenly Father, You tell us that You show love to a thousand generations of those who love You and keep Your commandments. (Exodus 20: 6) So I pray that my grandchild _____ will not be led astray to worship any other image of a being or thing. That they would not even be enticed to follow after anything besides You.

Do not let _____ become so enthralled with any idea, organization or false religion or their images, that they bow down and sacrifice their time, energy, money, or talent to it. That would be idolatry.

I pray that You would help my grandchild recognize and reject any false gods portrayed in any way through school, sports, advertising, society, or social media. Help _____ stand up to social pressure when friends are going the wrong way, chasing or worshipping the environment, money, popularity, success, or anything besides You.

Worship of other gods might look like innocent entertainment. Keep _____ from wrong things that would lead them into the occult like Tarot cards, Ouija boards, horoscopes, fortune tellers, channeling, seances, or those who seek to speak to the dead or to summon the devil.

Help me set a good example to _____ in how I live; passionate about You, putting you first, above the logos of cars, sports teams, beer labels or political parties. And help me teach them by example, how to love and honor You, by submitting myself to Your will, and worshipping You alone.

Father, let my grandchild _____ grow in wisdom, in stature and in favor with You and man. Amen

3rd Commandment—Honor God's Name

Ex 20:7, ***You shall not misuse the name of the Lord your God...***

Heavenly Father, in teaching my grandchild _____ to love and respect You, let them learn that even Your name is holy. And not to be spoken lightly. Your name is power, healing, and the name by which we all must be saved. So do not let them use it as a swear word, or make it common in their speech without the honor and respect it deserves.

I pray that profanity and disrespect for You would not be tolerated in my grandchild's family or their school or in their friends' language. Let me set a good example in my own speech, even when I'm angry. If I slip up, let me go to them and apologize, asking for forgiveness and sharing how it was wrong.

Bring a desire for creative use of language, choosing words that are good, lovely, noble and encouraging, skipping past profane words, and choosing even to steer away from coarse language and phrases.

Give my grandchild _____ the courage to set a good example by their own words and actions, speaking up when offended by others' wrongful use of Your name. Bring _____ godly role models of good speech when they are young so they learn at an early age to honor Your name. And increase their vocabulary so my grandchild can say what they mean without the desire or need to resort to profanity.

As _____ grows and is potentially exposed to differing values of speech, help them make a personal decision not to follow the pattern of the language of the world, but choose to be reverent with their choice of words and respectful of You in their speech.

Father, let my grandchild _____ grow in wisdom, in stature and in favor with You and man. Amen

DAY 25

4th Commandment—Honor the Sabbath

Exodus 20:8, ***Remember the Sabbath by keeping it holy.***

Heavenly Father, when You created the heavens and the earth, You set night and day divisions and a pattern of time for work and rest. You knew us so well, that we would need to rest, so You gave us a rhythm and made that day of rest "holy." It is to be set apart, different from the other days.

You created man and woman on the sixth day so our first full day was the seventh, a day of rest. That day empowers and strengthens us to face the rest of the week. And so our grandchildren need a rhythm too. Help us as grandparents model that. It's so easy to be busy all the time and fill each day with activities that drain us of physical, mental and emotional energy.

Father, let my grandchild _____'s family life and home also reflect a rhythm that honors You. As they make decisions about school, sports and other activities, remind them to consider a day of rest once a week. Guide them to see how much better weeks go when there is a day of rest.

And not just refraining from regular activity, let it truly be a day of worship and rest. Whether in a formal church setting, let the Sabbath be a day when _____ can relax and enjoy being who they are. Let rest recharge their growing body and feed their soul. Give them time for reflection on who You are and show _____ how You are working in their life.

In this relaxed time, make _____ mindful of acknowledging and thanking You as they grow in their awareness of their Creator. Let a Sabbath day be truly different from other days of the week.

Father, let my grandchild _____ grow in wisdom, in stature and in favor with You and man. Amen

DAY 26

5th Commandment—Honor Parents

Exodus 20:12, ***Honor your father and your mother, so that you may live long in the land the Lord your God is giving you.***

Heavenly Father, my grandchild _____ comes into this world knowing nothing, and has so much to learn about the world around them. But even in that state, as they grow and learn, most seem resistant, even rebellious to obey the authorities in their lives. It seems as soon as someone tells them "No" that's the way they want to go.

While most rules are set for my grandchild's protection, children can see them as restrictions and push against them at almost any age. I pray that my grandchild _____ would recognize, appreciate and obey these rules set for their protection, instead of questioning them. And without having to learn the hard way, through accident or tragedy, that the rule was meant to help and to shield them from harm.

And that as they grow, help _____ trust the authorities in their life: parents, grandparents, teachers, coaches, police and other first responders. Beyond that, Father, protect _____ from any who would take advantage of them or misuse their own authority for evil or harm. As authority figures come into _____'s life, give those people a strong sense of accountability and integrity. If there are any who would harm a child, expose them and remove them from those positions of authority.

When _____ reaches the age of being able to have input into the family or personal rules, give them wisdom to recognize and accept concern for their safety and the limits that are appropriate for their family needs at the time. And be willing to accept and honor their parents in word and deed.

As this is the only commandment that includes a blessing, let it be evident in _____'s life, every time they choose to listen, be humble, slow to speak, and in every way they show respect to their parents.

Father, let my grandchild _____ grow in wisdom, in stature and in favor with You and man. Amen

DAY 27

6th Commandment—Honor Life

Exodus 20:13, ***You shall not murder.***

Heavenly Father, I pray that my grandchild _____ will respect and honor life. And will encourage others to do the same. You say if we even harbor angry thoughts or say "Raca" that we have committed murder in our hearts. So I pray for peace in the heart and mind of my grandchild.

Teach _____ how to take captive any angry or murderous thoughts they might have and not act on them against a person or an animal or pet. Show them that positive actions and words can diminish and nullify conflict. Father, protect _____ from television, movie, music, video games and social media that would present murder or harming someone else or an animal for any reason as acceptable.

Protect my grandchild _____ from thoughts of suicide and let them never entertain thoughts of or make plans to take their own life. Let _____ feel Your love every day of their life, and let that give them hope, no matter what circumstances they have to deal with.

I pray that my grandchild would consider life so precious and valuable from God, that from conception, abortion would not be considered as a reasonable option. Help _____ choose life! No matter the social or cultural climate. Give them strength to stand up for godly values, and for life.

A similar attitude for euthanasia, whether young or old, sick or well, rich or poor, give _____ a strong belief that life comes from You. And that You determine the number of days, and that decision is Yours alone.

Spur this respect for life towards animals as well, learning and showing care towards pets. Let the boys be slow to point BB guns at a bird, let the girls go easy dressing up the family dog. Let _____ have a heart to protect life, in all forms, from the lowliest sparrow to unpopular kids talking about self-harm. Let them clearly see and protect the life You've given this earth, in all its many forms.

Father, let my grandchild _____ grow in wisdom, in stature and in favor with You and man. Amen

DAY 28

7th Commandment—Honor Marriage

Exodus 20:14, ***You shall not commit adultery.***

Heavenly Father, I pray that You would protect my grandchild _____ from sexual abuse or any kind of inappropriate sexual behavior. I pray for moral purity in them, and for moral purity in their role models and all those around them in positions or authority.

Let _____ grow in an understanding of Your perfect, unconditional agape love that protects, encourages and lifts them up. Let them receive Your love that accepts them so they do not look for love and acceptance in wrong places. Keep them safe from, and teach them to refrain from, the kind of talk and relationships that would degrade love.

As _____ grows, I pray that that when they see or hear love degraded to lust in any form of entertainment—movies, TV, printed material, music, or on the playground—they would turn away from it and refuse to watch or listen.

Even in school, I ask for godly standards in their sex education material and in its presentation. Let the realistic costs and unintentional consequences of immorality be presented. And let _____ see and understand the reasons for sexual purity in their own lives, regardless of the choices others around them make.

Provide openness and opportunities for _____ to approach their parents or even me for honest, meaningful conversations, support, encouragement, and guidance in these areas of marriage, sex, and purity.

In time, as situations present themselves, I pray that _____ would, recognize and resist the temptations that might lead to pornography or circumstances where they are in "over their heads" and make unwise decisions regarding intimacy and sex.

Help them resist pornography in all its forms and whoever or whatever might tempt them towards it. Give them the courage to say no and the ability to turn away from sexual sin. Make a way of escape for _____ when it is necessary to flee immorality.

Let _____ see the value of a loving marriage relationship in our family. Remind us to talk about and show how much we love each other, and value marriage, faithfulness, respect for one another. Let my marriage reflect our love and respect towards each other in simple, everyday ways, and the impact it has on the other person. Let _____ see this clearly and want it dearly for their own future self.

Father, bring a godly mate for my grandchild who will love You, and love _____. Let their love be sweet and all You intend it to be for married couples, regardless of the cultural and society values of the times. Let their marriage be sexually fulfilling, and the emotional, spiritual and physical bonds strong enough to withstand extramarital sexual temptation.

Father, let my grandchild _____ grow in wisdom, in stature and in favor with You and man. Amen

Reflect, Show & Share

How are you doing so far? If you have been able to be consistent in praying this week—good for you!

If not, what has gotten in your way?

______

How can you remedy that?

______

If you missed any prayers, just pick up tomorrow where you left off. During your prayer time has God shown you anything new about Himself? About your grandchild, or about yourself?

______

______

→Share the Bible story of the Ten Commandments or watch the movie.

→If married, show your wedding ring and photos of your wedding. Share what marriage means to you, to their parents, and what Anniversaries are and how they celebrate

→Show them wedding photos of any relatives they have and tell the ways their weddings were special, where they were, how everyone dressed, special food or activities

Your ideas to Reflect, Show or Share

______

______

______

______

______

______

______

______

I got to be at my grandparents 50th Wedding Anniversary. It was a big party where the whole family and some good friends gathered at their home. I was only three, and very small, so it was a lot of big people for me to be around. A special photographer showed up and took a picture that went in the local newspaper.

There was a specially decorated cake which I wasn't allowed to touch. And special dishes and glasses were brought out, which I was also not allowed to touch. And my mother, pregnant with my younger sister, was taking care of lots of details at the party.

When the party was all over, my grandmother Minnie came and put me on her lap in the big rocking chair—the one that was so heavy I couldn't rock it myself. She had brought the family photo albums out of the glass cabinet to spread on our laps and we looked through them all—her stopping occasionally to tell me funny and wonderful stories about the pictures and the people in them. All Polaroids, and only in black and white, stuck on to black pages with tiny white corner stickers.

I don't remember all the stories, and I haven't seen the photos in years—my older cousin has them all for now, but I do remember how lost I felt at the party, but how "found" and loved I felt when she took me on her lap into that big rocking chair.

8th Commandment—Honor Ownership

Exodus 20:15, ***You shall not steal.***

Heavenly Father, I pray for my grandchild _____ to grow up with the godly values expressed in these Ten Commandments. Let _____ receive simple, clear instruction of what is right and what is wrong. *You shall not steal* seems a simple enough concept to understand. And yet it almost seems to be human nature to be selfish and want things we don't have.

I pray for honesty and integrity in _____. That they would respect personal property and not take things that belong to others. Early on, teach them to share what they have and play cooperatively with others. As they grow, help _____ be content with what they have, and meet their needs so they do not have to do without.

Let _____ be honest in school and at work, including not cheating by "stealing" answers or work from others. Bring them godly friends and role models who would not exhibit or tolerate that behavior either. Teach them to be financially accountable and upright when dealing with others.

Father, teach _____ life lessons that will stay with them even if it hurts at the time. With all these commandments, cement in their mind the value behind each one, why it is wrong and the price they pay. Let them see the negative and harmful results, even the pain and suffering caused by lying or stealing or not respecting life.

When they sin, let them learn the consequences early in life. If they cheat on a test or steal a candy bar, or hurt someone, even accidentally, let them get caught and pay the price, learning this lesson well, the first and only time."

Father, do not let others not "steal" my grandchild's mental, emotional or spiritual growth, by putting false concepts in their teaching. Protect my grandchild from all ungodly influences that would seek to steal their honesty, integrity, identity, purity, creativity, innocence, or God-given character.

Father, let my grandchild _____ grow in wisdom, in stature and in favor with You and man. Amen

DAY 30

9th Commandment—Honor Truth

Exodus 20:16, ***You shall not give false testimony against your neighbor.***

Heavenly Father, I pray my grandchild _____ would grow up valuing and demonstrating honesty. Not lying is a simple enough concept to understand, and yet again, it seems human nature to want to say anything to protect ourselves or cover up any perceived wrongdoing on our part.

I pray _____ will value truth-telling—to their parents, among their friends and in their relationships. And that _____ will seek the truth in all things and will recognize Your truth as absolute. Let Your truth be the guiding principle for _____'s speech and life.

There are many reasons people lie. Demonstrate to _____ a good line between "telling stories" and telling the truth. When caught in a lie, help _____ face the truth and come clean, without becoming angry or defensive, or continuing the lie.

You, Lord, have set the standard we are to live by. And how we are to deal with others in this commandment. Help _____ learn to speak the truth in love so there is no need to lie. Show them clearly and early in life the negative consequences lying can cause—distrust, hurt feelings, anger, and broken relationships.

Encourage honesty to be a foundational aspect of _____'s relationships. In the family, among friends, and later in their closest and most intimate relationships, show _____ the freedom of being able to be open with their circumstances, their feelings, their joys, dreams, and even fears in a way that strengthens the bonds they have with people.

In court we place our hand on Your Bible and swear to tell the truth. Help me model truth-telling to my grandchild. Not just in court, but in everyday dealings with each other and everyone else.

Father, let my grandchild _____ grow in wisdom, in stature and in favor with You and man. Amen

DAY 31

10th Commandment—Honor Contentment

Exodus 20:17, ***You shall not covet...***

Heavenly Father, teach my grandchild _____ to trust You completely with all their needs. And to accept what comes from You with gratitude. I ask You to meet all _____'s needs; physical, mental, emotional, social, psychological, and spiritual so they will not go to other people or places seeking what they need.

When _____ sees what others have, let them also see and appreciate the benefits of the way they are being raised and be thankful for the home, parents, siblings, friends, opportunities and lifestyle they have. Do not let jealousy grow in _____ so that they covet others' toys, games, clothing, cars, money, standard of living, athletic or academic achievements, talents, abilities, or spiritual gifts.

Remind _____ that a person's value is not what they have. Despite advertising and marketing which promote comparison and envy, a person's worth is not what toys they have, what kind of car they drive, their clothes or outward successes. Let _____ learn that comparing ourselves is not wise at any age (2 Corinthians 10:12) and that envy rots the bones! (Proverbs 14:30)

Do not let _____ allow jealousy and coveting to lead to bitterness, anger and depression. Keep them from self-destructive attitudes and behaviors that could negatively affect their physical and mental health. And prevent them from becoming rebellious, with acting out behavior or violence.

Show _____ examples of gratitude and thankfulness to follow. Let me be a godly example of gratefulness for all You have blessed me with. Help me find ways to demonstrate to my grandchild my thanks for what You have given me and how to be happy for others when they are blessed.

Let _____ also find it in their heart to celebrate others' successes, even when it's hard.

Father, let my grandchild _____ grow in wisdom, in stature and in favor with You and man. Amen

DAY 32

Direction

Psalm 32:8 ***I will instruct you and teach you in the way you should go; I will counsel you with my loving eye on you.***

Heavenly Father, I pray that You would make my grandchild _____ sensitive to Your perspective on opportunities that arise and challenges that present themselves. Give _____ supernatural discernment and insight into issues when faced with choices.

Keep _____ from running headlong into decisions based only on what they think they see with their physical eyes or understand from their perspective. Show _____ how to set godly priorities. Help them take the time to recognize what is important and what is not. Not just what seems urgent at the time.

Teach _____ how to ask You for direction in prayer and listen for Your answer. You speak in so many ways; give _____ a clear understanding of Your direction. And confirm it with scripture or a word from a wise Christian in their life. As _____ seeks Your wisdom, give them enough light to see the next step to take, and the direction to go.

Show _____ where You are at work, opening or closing a door with finances, career, relationships, family, health, ministry, and needs in every area of their life. And how to be bold to walk through those doors You open, and honor those doors You close.

When _____ has confirmation of the direction You would lead, help them "Be strong and courageous…not afraid…or discouraged…" for You will be with them wherever they go. (Joshua 1:9)

Father, let my grandchild _____ grow in wisdom, in stature and in favor with You and man. Amen

DAY 33

Work Ethic

Ecclesiastes 9:10, ***Whatever your hand finds to do, do it with all your might.***

Heavenly Father, don't let my grandchild _____ be afraid of hard work. Whether putting a good effort into a hobby, learning a new skill, studying, or perfecting an artistic performance, let _____ recognize that "you get out of something what you put into it." And that hard work pays off.

As _____ grows, many things may come easily and be fun to do. But let _____ also see the value in spending time and effort learning to do something the right way. And when something doesn't come easy help them see the growth and maturity in themselves and the value of improving their skill.

When there is a quick way that cuts corners and produces a second-rate outcome, show _____ that doing your best is worth the effort. And that other people notice. And that You notice. Encourage _____ to work at whatever they do with all their heart, as if doing it for You. (Colossians 3:23)

When opportunity comes to have a job, impress on _____ how to respect the job and the people they work with and work for. Teach them at home and on the job how to honor their commitment to do their best.

Whether a job like baby-sitting, a chore like being in charge of feeding the fish, a hobby, or just doing something for fun, let _____ see that if it's worth doing, it's worth doing well.

Father, let my grandchild _____ grow in wisdom, in stature and in favor with You and man. Amen

DAY 34

Encouragement

Isaiah 41:10, So do not fear, for I am with you; do not be dismayed, for I am your God. I will strengthen you and help you; I will uphold you with my righteous right hand.

Heavenly Father, bring the emotional and spiritual encouragement and support that my grandchild _____ needs to meet the challenges and trials they face daily, as well as the more difficult burdens that arise as they grow.

Fill _____ with the motivation and courage they need to be bolstered up, energized to go forward mentally, emotionally, and spiritually. Open their eyes to see how You are working in their life, around them and for them. Open their ears to Your and others' words of love, support, and encouragement.

You created _____. And You knew beforehand the purpose of their life, the places they will go, and the perils they will face. You carefully fashioned _____ and have prepared them to handle, with Your help, whatever they need to face now and all throughout their life.

Encourage them with scripture and make Your promises personal, like this:

> You have carried _____ since their birth...You will continue to be with _____ and sustain them, even when _____ has gray hairs. You will always carry _____; You will always sustain _____; You will always rescue _____.
>
> And when _____ keeps their mind focused on You, You will keep _____ in perfect peace. (Isaiah 46:3-4; 26:3)
>
> You are with _____ always. You will always be holding their hand; You will guide _____ with Your counsel, and take them into glory...You are the strength of _____'s heart and their portion forever. (Psalm 73:23-26)

At some point, inspire _____ to keep a notebook or make a timeline of when You have helped or encouraged them. Let the remembrance of those examples of Your faithfulness build their faith and trust in You. And let _____ observe courage in others facing similar challenges and learn from their mistakes and triumphs. Let those testimonies encourage _____.

Give me opportunities to share stories with my grandchild: Bible stories of Old Testament heroes and of Jesus. Stories of my childhood adventures when I was awesome, and even when I failed, and the lessons I learned. Stories that encourage them even in those failings, especially if they are similar to something _____ is going through.

Remind me to tell when and how You have encouraged me in the past and all You're doing in my life now. Prompt me to share promises from scripture, how You are true to Your promises. And that _____ is not alone in their trials. That they have personal access to the God of the universe who has limitless resources. And that in Your faithfulness, You will provide what _____ needs.

Father, let my grandchild _____ grow in wisdom, in stature and in favor with You and man. Amen

DAY 35

Reject Entitlement or Victim Mentality

2 Timothy 1:7, ***For the Spirit God gave us does not make us timid, but gives us power, love and self-discipline.***

Heavenly Father, help my grandchild _____ grow in humility, being content with what You provide for them and accepting responsibility for themselves. Give _____ a strong sense of accountability. And bring godly people into their life who will hold them accountable for their actions, words, and attitudes.

Do not let _____ develop an attitude of entitlement. Don't let it create a barrier that keeps out personal responsibility, right behavior and a godly perspective. Entitlement brings manipulation and scheming as people try to get what they feel they deserve or are owed. Don't let my grandchild _____ live by this morality that allows them to do whatever they feel is right for them, or whatever they can get away with to get what they want.

On the other extreme, do not let _____ fall into a victim mentality, refusing to accept responsibility for their own actions. When hurting, it can be so easy to fall into apathy or to blame others. Protect my grandchild from this thinking that robs them of their ability to make wise decisions and take charge of their life.

Father, as _____ grows, show them how to take in the power You have given them—that spirit of power and love and a sound mind that will help them overcome evil. (2 Timothy 1:7) Allow the power of Your love for _____ to overcome these destructive mentalities. Strengthen them to live their life as an "Overcomer" in every age and stage of their development.

Father, let my grandchild _____ grow in wisdom, in stature and in favor with You and man. Amen

Reflect, Show & Share

Almost there! You're doing great! —good for you!

If you missed any prayers, just pick up where you left off
During your prayer time has God shown you anything new about Himself? About your grandchild, or about yourself?

→Read yourself, or google 5 Love Languages for kids and plan a way to speak to them in their love language:

Physical touch—cuddle on a sofa or rocking chair to read a book, watch a movie or video, hugs, high fives, rub their back or hands

Words of Affirmation—speak how much you love them or how well they've done something, or write it in notes or cards, text those words

Quality Time—make eye contact when you see them or Zoom together, have date time, bake together, walk together, play games, teach them

Gifts—make something for them, find personalized gifts, give small inexpensive things that fit their interests, mail them a small package

Acts of Service—cook just for them, help them with homework or practice for a sport, volunteer with them, fix something broken of theirs

→Show the result of your work on a goal you had and share what steps you had to do to meet that goal, the time it took, like building or growing something, making a collection

♥ Share about the work it takes and the satisfaction you feel of a job well done, the accomplishment you feel when completing a project

→if it's possible, find a goal for the two of you and plan a project, build a model, plant a window box garden,

→let them "help" you work on something.

Your ideas to Reflect, Show or Share

Maw Maw and Paw Paw moved from the farm into town and opened and ran a grocery store with gas pumps in front. People could gas up and then come inside to shop. And their home was connected to the back of the store.

When we visited I could play in the house part or play in the store, but the part that always enthralled me was the candy counter. Most of the candy was behind a glass-front case that the cash register sat on. When people paid, they could name their preference and Paw Paw would reach inside and deliver the sweet goodness.

Sometimes he'd let me reach in for the candy and then push the button on the register that made it ding while he bagged up the groceries. I felt so grown up when I could "help" him.

At the end of one of our yearly visits, he gave my sister and me each a paper sack and said we could fill it with anything we wanted from the store! My eyes got huge as the joy spread over my face and I raced to the candy counter.

I got those little bags of salted peanuts that you can pour into your bottle of Coke to enjoy the sweet, salty flavors together as you drank from the bottle and chewed the nuts. I grabbed several of the Bazooka bubble gum packets that came with a comic strip. And wrapped butterscotch candies, gumballs, Pixie Stix, Necco wafers, and a Bit-O-Honey.

With my bag full of my own choices I got in the car and waved good-bye, feeling like I had been given the biggest and best treat of my life.

It was only decades later, as I made my own kids' lunches, that I realized how small the sack was that I had been given. Probably smaller than the lunch sacks I was filling. But that day, allowed to make my own choices, to fill what seemed a limitless bag, I felt so special and valued and loved.

DAY 36

Keep from Evil

Psalm 1:1, ***Blessed is the one who does not walk in step with the wicked or stand in the way that sinners take or sit in the company of mockers.***

Heavenly Father, lead my grandchild _____ to know right from wrong. Let _____ feel the love You have for them and the care You take with them. Protect them with Your power, from evil in their comings and goings. Give _____ positive examples of people doing good, honoring You; and opportunities for them to do the same.

If _____ is around evil, let them feel uncomfortable and run from those people or activities or places, literally and figuratively. If they stumble upon evil, open their eyes to see the harm and the trap before they get drawn into it.

Don't let _____ follow the example of people who take Your name in vain or deny Your presence or Your work here on earth. Stop _____ from following the crowd and participating in activities that expose them to wickedness or mock You with their words, actions, or attitudes.

Father, do not let _____ be lured into evil or be tempted by the temporary pleasures of evil. But let them see what is good and right and just. And that the devil who tempts them will trap them and take them farther than they ever meant to go. Even let _____ learn from the painful lessons and experiences of others that evil does not pay, and that it will cost them more than they could anticipate.

Let them love what You love, let them hate what You hate.

At whatever age and level of _____'s spiritual maturity, let them sense You watching over them and remember that they are Yours. And let that be a powerful deterrent, and an awesome reassurance.

Father, let my grandchild _____ grow in wisdom, in stature and in favor with You and man. Amen

DAY 37

Heart of Kindness

Ephesians 4:32, ***Be kind and compassionate to one another...***

Heavenly Father, teach my grandchild _____ to be kind and compassionate. You are the best example. Your free gift of mercy is withholding judgement or punishment that is deserved. And Your grace has granted _____ benefits they could never earn.

Father show _____ where You have extended them grace and mercy throughout their life. Let them see where, by Your favor and out of Your love, You have blessed them. And in turn, teach _____ how to share that blessing.

As they grow, make _____ aware of others around them needing mercy, kindness, or grace from them. Embolden _____ to withhold judgment and extend mercy, even when they might have a right to do otherwise.

You have commanded us to love our neighbor as ourselves. Open _____'s eyes to see who is hurting right where they are. Help them look beyond any differences and see when people are grieving or in need. Not just people who look or think like them. But give _____ Your heart to help them however they can.

Father, refine _____'s heart to be a loving, caring person who brings honor to Your name. Enable their eyes, their ears to see You at work around them. And to join You in caring for people.

Help _____ grow in awareness that You are with them wherever they go. And let that be a powerful deterrent to keep them behaving honorably. And an awesome reassurance that You see their honorable way of living.

Father, let my grandchild _____ grow in wisdom, in stature and in favor with You and man. Amen

DAY 38

Healing

Jeremiah 30:17a ***'But I will restore you to health and heal your wounds,' declares the Lord...***

Heavenly Father, so many things in life can cause us to be hurt or have weaknesses physically, emotionally, or spiritually. Move into any places of brokenness my grandchild _____ has in their life. Make them strong physically, mentally, emotionally and spiritually. Wherever there are broken places, speak Your life and Your healing.

Where there is disease or damage, speak health into their bones, organs, their whole body. And heal those emotional places where people have disappointed _____, or let them down, or even caused them pain.

Broken places can be weaknesses where _____ is vulnerable to temptation into sin and believing lies. Heal any spiritual wounds where they have believed lies that have kept You at a distance. And while You are healing those areas, protect and encourage _____.

Protect _____ by hedging them in, in front and back, along their sides, above and below so that no evil power can get in and lead them farther away from You. Encourage _____ as You are healing them by bringing someone alongside them who will give wise counsel, and by checking their attitudes and guiding them into godly decisions.

Give _____ faith to trust what You say: that You love them and that Your love is greater than whatever difficulty they're going through. Spread Your protection over their body, mind and spirit. Thank You for being their Jehovah Rapha: their Healer.

Father, let my grandchild _____ grow in wisdom, in stature and in favor with You and man. Amen

DAY 39

Complete the Good Work

Philippians 1:3-6, ***I thank my God every time I remember you. In all my prayers...being confident of this, that he who began a good work in you will carry it on to completion until the day of Christ Jesus.***

Heavenly Father, I praise You for the unique and special way You have created my grandchild _____. I believe You have woven _____ together with the traits, aptitudes, personality, talents, and gifts exactly as You desired.

Help _____ see those unique and special ways You created them. And how to use those qualities to bring honor and glory to You. Open their eyes to opportunities You provide. And give them courage to act, and the inspiration they need to keep at it and not give up. Encourage them. And help them find joy in using the gifts and talents You have given them in all stages of their life.

I also understand that the world and the evil one will seek to destroy the good and waylay the purposes You have for _____. I trust that You are stronger and more powerful than any other influences, and that You have promised to bring to completion the good work You have begun in _____.

Father, derail the plans that the evil one and the world make against _____. Be at work in their life to bring them to a saving knowledge of You and a willingness to obey You and whatever You call them to. Whether a ministry, a vocation, a passion, or in the way they impact other's lives, finish the work You have begun in _____.

Father, let my grandchild _____ grow in wisdom, in stature and in favor with You and man. Amen

DAY 40

Lay Them on the Altar

Genesis 22:2, ***Then God said, "Take your son, your only son, whom you love—Isaac—and go to the region of Moriah. Sacrifice him there as a burnt offering on a mountain I will show you."***

Heavenly Father, I admit that no matter how deeply I love my grandchild _____ and want them to experience salvation and a joyful life, I cannot make it happen. Only You can do all that.

I am so grateful that You already know the good plan You have for _____'s life, to prosper them and not harm them, but to give _____ hope and a future. (Jeremiah 29:11)

Just as You commanded Abraham to lay Isaac on the sacrificial altar, I acknowledge that _____ is your child. They mean the world to me, so I lay _____ on the altar as a sacrifice to say that I acknowledge Your control of their life; and all the factors that affect their attitudes and decision-making processes. I surrender my hopes and dreams for them, and whatever hold or control I may have imagined I have over them and I leave them in Your capable and loving hands.

I know You will protect Your precious child _____ from evil. Thank You in advance for directing their path to use the gifts and talents You have given them to allow them to fulfill the purpose You created them for. As the stars shine bright in the sky, shine brightly in _____'s life and heart and spirit to dispel any darkness around them—whatever the source.

I give You thanks and praise in advance, and wait, anticipating the miracles You will work in _____'s life.

Father, let my grandchild _____ grow in wisdom, in stature and in favor with You and man. Amen

Reflect, Show & Share

You made it! 40 Days! —We are so proud of you!

During your 40 day prayer journey has God shown you anything new about Himself? About your grandchild, or about yourself?

And if so, how will you apply it to your life?

Your ideas to Reflect, Show or Share

It wasn't till after I had children that I began writing poems, songs, devotionals and prayers. I kept them to myself, too embarrassed to actually show them to anyone. Certainly not my husband, parents or friends.

When MawMaw moved into the nursing home, I began calling her every Sunday evening. I knew she was lonely and I wanted to encourage her to make new friends and give her a friendly voice to talk to. This went on for years.

In college, she sent homemade banana bread to my dorm. During college breaks I sometimes went to see her. It was only a few hours' bus ride and she'd let me drive her car and run errands for her. Even as an adult we were friends.

She was my "safe" person. I could say almost anything, and ask her almost anything. Maybe it was because I knew she loved me, maybe because it was less threatening to share by phone, but she was the first person I sang some of my songs to. And guess what? She loved them!

Not that she was a musician or would actually recognize talent. But she was a loving grandmother!

She encouraged me and helped me get to the point where I was ready to sing them to a friend—our music director. Before long I was singing my songs at Bible Study, and in our church services. And sharing devotions with others in a small booklet I had printed. And later, poems and prayers with other people—and now in books and on my blogs!

The love and encouragement of a grandparent should never be underestimated. Your role is important. Even the small things you do now are building into a relationship that will return amazing dividends if you don't give up.

You matter. You have an impact.

May the Lord bring you love and joy and peace, and prosper you all your days as you share His love and joy and peace with your precious grandchild and family. Amen

Thank You After 40 Days

Heavenly Father, thank You for this journey of praying for my grandchild _____ for 40 days. It is wonderful to have covered them in prayer so intentionally and consistently. Thank You for Your help in keeping me faithful on this journey. And for the things You have shown me and taught me while spending time with You.

Help me remember what You have shown me about You, and my grandchild, and about myself. Thank You for the things You have called to my mind from my experiences with my own grandparents. And what I can choose to repeat or avoid from them.

Remind me to make plans from the ideas You gave me that will fit with my relationship with _____ from the Show and Share.

Thank You too for all You have done in my grandchild _____'s life as Your power has been released there.

I continue to pray that You will make Your presence known and Your blessings felt in their life. That _____ will sense You at work, in large ways and in small ones. I am continually grateful that I can pray for You to effect Your will and Your purpose for _____. I lift my prayer for You to demonstrate to them that through salvation and blessing, You came to bring them an abundant life!

May _____ never ever forget that You are with them and that they are Your child. May that remembrance be a powerful deterrent and an awesome reassurance. I believe Your Word will not return void, and as I have prayed Your Word over _____ I am trusting that it will continue to bear fruit long after these 40 days have passed.

Thank You for hearing and answering my prayers—in ways that are above and beyond what I could ever ask for or even imagine. Show me if there is someone else I need to be praying for...even for myself. And be with me on that journey as well. Amen

APPENDICES

APPENDIX A

Prayers for Childhood through Adult Stages

Stage Prayer: Pregnancy

Heavenly Father, I first acknowledge that all life comes from You. That it is a gift, a blessing. Thank You for creating this miracle of life that is my grandchild. I ask for Your perfect will to be done in this pregnancy.

Father, You know that with just the thought of a new grandchild, my whole life has changed. I've made plans in my heart for the child to come, ordering my thoughts around the possibilities of their existence—birth, growth, what they will look like, what their experiences will be… My world is turned upside down with the hopes of grandparenthood or a new grandchild.

As this pregnancy grows, protect it there. Let all the physical and hormonal things that need to happen, happen normally. Let the mother's body respond as You fearfully and wonderfully created it, to protect and nurture a baby. Let this grandchild grow and develop in the womb without complications. Bless the mother with good health, energy, and stamina to carry this precious child.

Protect the parents in this time of change and expectancy. Let them grow closer to each other and closer to You. Prepare their hearts to receive this blessing. If concerns arise, and there are often many concerns regarding lifestyle, places to live, jobs, expenses, health, let them turn to You, knowing that You are bigger than any problem. Let this be a time of building and growing their faith in You.

When the time comes for delivery of this precious child, be present with the whole family welcoming this new life. Give the parents the courage to embrace parenthood, regardless of the circumstances. Provide for their safety and needs. Arrange for the help they need in necessary medical support, knowledge of what to expect, and stress management skills for labor. Give the mother the physical and emotional strength to last through labor and then deliver Your miracle of life.

Thank You for the blessing of this grandchild. Amen

Stage Prayer: Infancy

Heavenly Father, I praise You for the precious life of this beautiful grandbaby _____. What an amazing gift to see _____ and hold them and get to know them. After months of wondering, I now get to see what they look like, sound like, feel like when I hold and cuddle them in my arms. I am incredibly blessed.

Father, protect my grandchild _____ from childhood illnesses, injuries, and accidents. If there are allergies or specific special needs, prepare the parents to get the medical expertise and training they need to address every issue that requires special care. Strengthen _____'s immune systems and help them avoid any medical complications in their growth.

Watch over them while they sleep. Let _____ sleep well for their own benefit to be healthy and alert, and for their parents' benefit so everyone gets the sleep they need. Guide _____'s growth, helping them make progress in all the ways a baby needs to develop. Strengthen their digestive system so they get the nourishment they need. Help their bones and muscles grow strong. And their coordination develop well.

Help my grandchild's mind grow sharp, and their hearing and sight be good to take in all the things of this amazing world You have brought them into. As _____ matures and learns to crawl, walk and talk, help us all provide the physical, mental, sensory and relational stimulation and encouragement they need for proper development.

Provide for _____'s safety in their newly babyproofed home. Even in my own home, help me be mindful of any dangerous areas when they come to visit so that nothing will harm them while here. Let there be happy times of interaction as we welcome this baby into our family.

Thank You for the blessing of this grandchild. Amen

Stage Prayer: Child

Heavenly Father, I praise You for the growth and development I see in my grandchild _____. I continue to ask for Your protection over _____, physically, mentally, emotionally, psychologically, and spiritually.

Help _____ adjust to the changes around them and the changes taking place within them. When the family grows or makes changes in jobs or moving that affect _____, provide the support for understanding and coping with what's happening. Bring friends and family members alongside to make any necessary transitions easier.

As _____ begins school, bring teachers who will take the time to learn how _____ learns best. And bring friends who will be there to eat lunch with, play on the playground with and make learning and school more fun. Where there are difficulties that challenge my grandchild, bring the help that's needed, whether physical/medical, professional, educational, psychological, emotional or spiritual.

Since grandchildren see everything we do, help me remember to be aware of my own speech, actions, and how I display my attitudes as I spend time with _____. Let me notice their positive behaviors, gifts or talents, and find ways I can encourage and support those. And if I see behaviors or something that concerns me, give me wisdom to know what to do.

Along with physical and mental growth at school, allow opportunities for activities that will benefit _____'s social skills. Give _____ the chance to try out hobbies or sports, team activities, music lessons or outdoor experiences.

As a grandparent, I can play games and do activities with _____ that will teach life lessons and drive home values, like honesty, humility, cooperation, sharing, getting along, winning gracefully, losing gracefully. And perhaps help them learn from mistakes they make when they've done something wrong like broke something, stole a candy bar, hurt someone accidentally, or carelessly played too rough and hurt an animal.

Help me be the safe person they can come to spilling their hearts and guilt to, who can give wisdom in the moment. And at the same time remind them they are loved and forgiven. And even when the lessons hurt, can help them find restoration that will cement a life lesson that saves them from a bigger sin and shame in the future.

Let _____ discover what they're good at, what they enjoy, and focus on those things. Don't let them stress and worry over things they can't do, but bring resources to _____ that will encourage and develop the gits and talents, abilities and skills You 've given them.

And provide for their spiritual growth with a community of people who love and worship You. Open and grow _____'s understanding of who You are through the Bible, godly lessons appropriate for their age, living examples of godly living, and Your own personal communication with them.

Thank You for the blessing of this grandchild. Amen

Stage Prayer: Youth

Heavenly Father, I give You praise for the way You are growing my grandchild _____. Thank You for the physical and mental growth over these years. And thank You for the emotional and spiritual maturity I see. Give them a desire to honor and obey their parents and become a help to their family. In praying that _____ grow in wisdom and stature and in favor with You and man, show me how I can be part of their development.

I may not be a teacher, but show me when there are opportunities to share with them. Help me tune in to when there are teachable moments that will help them learn in school—subjects I may know something about, or ways to help them learn. Teach _____ good study habits so learning is easier. And when the schools are teaching things that go against our spiritual beliefs, give me the words to open discussions in positive ways that allow _____ to think about and process what they're hearing.

I may not be a coach, but provide opportunities where I can give my grandchild confidence in their appearance without criticism. Help me share the importance of taking good care of the body You have given them. Let us share fun physical activities that can increase their strength and agility, like arm wrestling, shooting hoops, or riding bikes. Or find games and projects to do together that stress movement and get us outdoors.

And in the activity, make time to talk about making wise decisions about eating right, getting the sleep they need, and exercising. If appropriate for our relationship, I can encourage _____ to stay away from drugs, smoking and making good decisions about sex. If not all these topics are right for us, then show me when to open my mouth, and when to close it and just listen.

I may not be a counselor, but let me be a sounding board for _____'s thoughts and ideas. Give them discernment in choosing friends, joining groups and picking activities in school. Bring godly options for _____ to choose from, especially as they grow to the age where parents aren't the number one source of advice anymore. Let them see godly role models and personal friends who exemplify kindness, courage, and respect for others. Help me choose activities with _____ that foster maturity and accepting responsibility—in the family and as they earn privileges.

I may not be a preacher, but give me opportunities to share my faith in natural, non-pushy ways. I can share my experiences with prayer and how You answered and made a difference in my life. I can tell about the ways I've seen You at work in my life, and encourage them to look for ways in their own life. I can talk to how the Bible has spoken to me when I needed encouragement or direction or hope.

Father, as life brings my grandchild opportunities, let them hear Your voice clearly behind them saying "This is the way, walk in it." (Isaiah 30:21) Help them choose wisely in making even small decisions that will influence their path in life. Give them wisdom and courage to dodge the traps the evil one sets for them with all the social pressure of irresponsible behavior like cheating, stealing, drinking, taking drugs, having sex, bullying or being violent, and worse.

Let them sense Your presence in real and tangible ways that creates a sense of personal accountability that acts as a powerful deterrent and a sense of awesome reassurance.

Thank You for the blessing of this grandchild. Amen

Stage Prayer: Young Adult

Heavenly Father, I praise You for allowing me to see my grandchild _____ almost grown. They are in a time of life that is so full of opportunities and changes that will affect the rest of their life. I am so grateful that You are with them and will never leave them. That You will always be available to them through Your Word, prayer, the Holy Spirit, and that You have placed people around them to provide godly advice as well. Father turn their heart to You.

They are enjoying more freedoms now. It started with having a bike, which gave them mobility. Then access to a car or truck for getting around on their own. Father, help _____ handle the responsibility that comes with those freedoms.

And while there is more freedom, there is also more pressure in studies—whether that means school and college classes or preparing for a career or a first job and having to learn all the responsibilities and duties that go along with that. Help them be clear-minded as they learn all they need to, to be successful in work and school. In all this pressure, Father, give _____ good times, faithful friends, godly role models, and a wise mentor.

Even if there have been serious relationships in _____'s life, now is the time when a more permanent marriage relationship may be considered. Help my grandchild take time to seek out someone with godly values, who loves You and will love them, and be faithful for that lifelong commitment. Encourage them to get to know one another, each other's families, values, hopes and dreams. Let there be discussions of their future together and what that would look like, sharing their views on children, money, and their faith.

Give my grandchild the focus they need to determine what they want to do with their life, and where they want to go. And then be able to say "No" to the things that don't fit their goals...regardless of what everyone else is doing.

The peer pressure gets even tougher now. _____ will need Your wisdom as they make decisions about where to live. If college or a job are in the picture, it may mean moving out of their parent's house and being on their own for the first time. And it becomes so easy to fall in line with what other young adults their age are doing, just to be part of the crowd and fit in. Help _____ get along with classmates, co-workers, the people of influence in their life. Protect and guide _____ in handling all these new pressures and influences.

If moving out, then help _____ be wise in choosing where to live, and with whom. Roommates can be a blessing or a challenge. Bring someone who can be like "iron sharpening iron", rather than iron poking iron. Teach _____ how to create a healthy living space with another person, how to get along, and set and respect appropriate boundaries. And let _____ carry the good habits and ways of living they learned at home to their new home, being respectful and accountable on their own.

Teach _____ to manage their own tasks and chores. It will fall on them to do their own laundry, wash their own dishes, prepare their own food, balance their own finances, and make hundreds of decisions about how to conduct their life. It will be up to them to choose their friends, pay their bills—that's a big one—and decide how to spend their free time. And now, on their own, _____ will decide how their relationship with You will look.

Many young adults have a crisis of faith, testing whether their faith is really their own, or just what they were brought up with. Father, be close to _____ at this time in their life. Let them sense Your presence, seek Your purpose for their life, and ask for Your wisdom to guide them. Put them in touch with a Bible believing and teaching church or Young Adult ministry. Help them find their way to You, and their place in You.

Thank You for the blessing of this grandchild. Amen

Stage Prayer: Adult

Heavenly Father, thank You for the great blessing of letting me see my grandchild _____ grow. You know how very much I love _____. I delight seeing them enjoy their successes. And seeing all the ways You have blessed them.

Even if they have not followed Your leading I still care deeply for them and pray that You will never let them go.

As You have promised to always be with them please continue to watch over their comings and goings. You know the best way to reach my grandchild right where they are. Father confront them when they sin. Bring them to repentance and draw them to a life of serving and worshiping You. It is my heart's desire to see them following and serving You.

Throughout _____'s life protect them from evil. Father lead them away from temptations that will draw them away from You. Give them wisdom for the decisions they make in choosing a lifelong mate, a career, a place to live, friends to fellowship with, and a Bible teaching church to be part of.

Continue to bring role models and mentors into their adult life. And help _____ learn from them how to live a godly and blessed life in the midst of this ungodly and corrupt world. Do not let their character be corrupted by declining social values, but surround them with godly influences that call them to a higher level of accountability to You. Let that be evident in their relationships, finances, business dealings and morality.

Give my grandchild a biblical world view that will guide them to seek Your perspective on issues and problems that may arise in their lifetime that I cannot even imagine. When they are confused bring them clarity. Remind them they can call on You at any time for anything because there is nothing too large or too small for You to handle. And that when they ask, You will always answer their prayer and give them the wisdom they need.

Continue to bring them Divine Appointments. When they have reached discouragement and come to the end of themselves and exhausted their abilities, show them that Your resources are limitless. That You can do immeasurably more than they can ask for or even imagine.

Father keep the joy of their salvation alive and fresh in my grandchild. Thank You for the blessing they have been in my life. Let the footprints that I leave on their life always lead them back to You. And be an inspiration to believe and trust in You. Amen

Thank You for the blessing of this grandchild. Amen

APPENDIX B

Confession and Repentance

Let God speak to you now and show you any sin you need to confess. Psalm 66:18 tells us if we cherish sin in our hearts, God won't listen to our prayers. Tell God you are willing to turn away from those things (which is repentance) and ask for His forgiveness.

1 John 1:9-10 tells us "If we confess our sins, He is faithful and righteous to forgive us our sins and to cleanse us from all unrighteousness. If we claim we have not sinned, we make Him a liar, and His word is not in us."

Ask God if there are sins of:

THOUGHT—impure, selfish, angry, fearful, jealous

ATTITUDE—prideful, judgmental, argumentative, lukewarm toward God

SPEECH—crude, inappropriate, grumbling, divisive, lies, half-truths

RELATIONSHIP—wrong or improper, physically or emotionally

Do you need to forgive someone? Do you need to ask for forgiveness?

As a husband: are you providing spiritual leadership, guiding and nurturing your wife?

As a wife: are you honoring and respecting your husband?

As parents: are you modeling godly behavior and attitudes and teaching your children in love?

As children or teens: are you respectful and obedient?

COMMISSION—things that you have done, actions you have taken

Have you done something you know is wrong?

Do you guard your eyes?

Have you exposed yourself to the occult?

Do you have habits that are harmful to your body—mind—spirit?

OMISSION—things you have failed to do

Has God prompted you to do something you haven't done?

Have you failed to do good when you could have?

SELF-RULE—rebellion, going your own way

Are you following God or going your own way?

Are you avoiding something He's told you to do?

Or are you still doing something He's told you not to?

APPRENDIX C

Spiritual Armor for Battle

Ephesians 6:10-18 ***Finally, be strong in the Lord and in his mighty power. Put on the full armor of God, so that you can take your stand against the devil's schemes. For our struggle is not against flesh and blood, but against the rulers, against the authorities, against the powers of this dark world and against the spiritual forces of evil in the heavenly realms. Therefore put on the full armor of God, so that when the day of evil comes, you may be able to stand your ground, and after you have done everything, to stand. Stand firm then, with the belt of truth buckled around your waist, with the breastplate of righteousness in place, and with your feet fitted with the readiness that comes from the gospel of peace. In addition to all this, take up the shield of faith, with which you can extinguish all the flaming arrows of the evil one. Take the helmet of salvation and the sword of the Spirit, which is the word of God.***

And pray in the Spirit on all occasions with all kinds of prayers and requests. With this in mind, be alert and always keep on praying for all the Lord's people.

We dress ourselves in the armor that Paul describes here. He wrote his letter to the Ephesians while he was in Rome, under house arrest, guarded by Roman soldiers. Every day, he saw men dressed in armor, bearing the insignia of their authority. The Holy Spirit must have inspired his analogy of a Christian "soldier."

Praying on the armor can be as simple as listing each piece and stating that you are putting it on and wearing it.

When we are praying for someone, or even ourselves, the devil doesn't like it. And even with his limited power here on earth, we can find ourselves under attack in ways that can lead us to feel discouraged, defeated, even want to give up.

But we rely on the fact that God's armor is the very best!

The **Belt of Truth** is a wide, tight band around the waist that holds pieces of the armor on as well as the sword. When we are wearing truth we can more easily recognize the lies the devil would tempt us to believe. We will not be mesmerized by half-truths or deceptions.

The **Breastplate of Righteousness** protects our heart and vital organs, a kind of forerunner of the bulletproof vest. It stops and deflects stabs and projectiles, keeping our heart and spirit from evil deceptions. Our righteousness comes from Jesus Christ. His blood paid the price for our sin and we gain the righteousness of the perfect life He lived. In that righteousness the devil cannot hold anything against us.

The **Shoes of the Gospel of Peace** help us walk in the Spirit. Putting on shoes is a sign of readiness and preparedness. With these we are ready to carry the Good News of salvation and peace into our relationships and whatever challenges we face. With our feet protected like this we will have traction even when we feel unsteady, and will be able to stand firm.

The **Shield of Faith** is not some puny little garbage can lid with a handle, but a head-to-toe protection, repelling the enemy's offensive weapons. When the shield was anointed with oil it would reflect the glare of the sun and blind the enemy. This shield covered a soldier from top to bottom, side to side and could join with others to form a wall of protection that would fend off an attacker while advancing in the field of battle.

Our faith in God protects us when the world or others tells us things are hopeless or cannot work out because we have the One True God who is all-knowing and all-powerful. We trust in His love for us and know that He has a plan for us, to give us hope and a future with Him in eternity. Every time He keeps a promise, or delivers us from some trouble, or stands with us in hardship, it builds or faith - strengthens our shields! And when we stand beside other believers in their faith, we are protected even more!

The **Helmet of Salvation** protects our head and identifies who we fight for. This helmet also protects our minds and helps guard our thoughts. The enemy would want to fill our minds with thoughts of doubt, fear and insecurity. But when thoughts and emotional responses are stirred up, we can hold them up to the light of truth: scripture. God's Word is the truth that will combat all that would discourage us.

And the **Sword of the Spirit** is God's Word, and strikes at the lies the devil would use to try and defeat us. We can use it to refute any lies the devil tries to get us to believe. We can pray it as part of our prayers. We can speak it out loud as an attack on the enemy. There is power in the Word of God.

Here is a sample prayer:

Heavenly Father, I come before you with thanks for the armor that You give me, which is the best. With the belt of truth fastened around my waist, I say that I will not believe the lies the devil would try to use to confuse me. Give me clarity and understanding. Help me see past what the world and others would tell me, to what you want to say to me.

I wear the helmet of salvation to guard my mind, and I take every thought captive to You. The breastplate of righteousness I place over my chest to protect my heart.

I wear the shoes of peace to say that I am ready to hear from You and to obey what You tell me to do and follow where You lead.

I take up my shield to repel all the arguments the evil one would send against me. And I take up the sword, the Word of God, as a weapon to help me stand firm against the devil's schemes.

Thank you for hearing my prayer. Amen.

APPENDIX D

Blessings and Scripture Prayers

Isaiah 11:2-3a

May the Spirit of the Lord rest on you, _____
The Spirit of wisdom and understanding
The Spirit of counsel and might
The Spirit of the knowledge and fear of the Lord
Delight yourself _____ in the fear of the Lord
('fear' meaning a reverence for the Lord)

Psalm 71: 1-8—For my grandchild

In you, LORD, show my grandchild _____ how to take refuge;
let them never be put to shame.
In your righteousness, rescue _____ and deliver them;
turn your ear to _____ and save them.
Be _____'s rock of refuge,
to which they can always go;
give the command to save _____,
because you are their rock and their fortress.
Deliver _____, my God, from the hand of the wicked,
from the grasp of those who are evil and cruel.
For you can be _____'s hope, Sovereign Lord,
their confidence since their youth.
From birth teach _____ how to rely on you;
you brought them forth from their mother's womb.
Let _____ ever praise you.
Let _____ become a sign to many;
you are their strong refuge.
Let _____'s mouth be filled with your praise,
declaring your splendor all day long.

Psalm 71:9-18—for Me

Do not cast me away when I am old;
do not forsake me when my strength is gone.
For my enemies speak against me;
those who wait to kill me conspire together. They say, "God has forsaken them;
pursue them and seize them,
for no one will rescue them."
Do not be far from me, my God;
come quickly, God, to help me.
May my accusers perish in shame;
may those who want to harm me
be covered with scorn and disgrace.
As for me, I will always have hope;
I will praise you more and more.
My mouth will tell of your righteous deeds,
of your saving acts all day long—
though I know not how to relate them all.
I will come and proclaim your mighty acts, Sovereign LORD;
I will proclaim your righteous deeds, yours alone.
Since my youth, God, you have taught me,
and to this day I declare your marvelous deeds.
Even when I am old and gray,
do not forsake me, my God,
till I declare your power to the next generation,
your mighty acts to all who are to come.

Colossians 1:9-14

I continually ask You, Lord God to fill _____ with the knowledge of Your will (not their own, or mine or anyone else's who might think to manipulate or control them)—(that _____ would know what Your good and perfect will is for them personally—first of all in relation to You, their Father—how You would have them use the gifts and talents You have given them, what their worship looks like, how they study to understand Your Word; next, in the roles they play in life—child, sibling, friend—in the relationships You have given them; last—what Your will in their life looks like in service through ministry, education or vocation) *through the wisdom and understanding that the Spirit gives* (not the wisdom of the world, or the logic of the mind, or the sense of the flesh), *so that _____ may live a life worthy of the Lord, and please him in every way: bearing fruit in every good work, growing in the knowledge of God.*

And that _____ *would be strengthened with all power according to His glorious might* (so not only physically when you need it, but mentally, emotionally, psychologically, and spiritually) *so that they may have great endurance and patience. And that _____ would joyfully give thanks to the Father, who has qualified them to share in His inheritance, with His holy people in the Kingdom of Light!*

Thanks be to You, Lord God *who has delivered _____ out of the dominion of darkness, and brought them into the Kingdom of Your beloved Son, in whom they have total redemption, the forgiveness of sins.* (May _____ be given the vision of the Holy Spirit today to have their eyes opened to the spiritual battle going on in their life. May they be given spiritual discernment to see where there is temptation, where there is oppression, where there are forces of the world, the flesh, and the evil one acting on them personally—in whatever form they take. May this knowledge give them the strength to fight these ungodly influences and overcome their power in _____'s life. So that _____ will be truly free in Your truth and be blessed by following You. Amen)

APPENDIX E

Lyrics to New and Improved

Paw Paw was a leader in a small west Texas town
People always liked him, they always came around
A farmer, then a grocer, and for a while he drove trucks of gasoline
When he came to Jesus, he was 34 years old
And when he was just 69 God rested his soul
But when people saw him walk that aisle to accept the Lord
It was a powerful scene

Chorus: New and Improved, he got Heaven above
New and Improved, but only by God's love
God's sacrifice for all, is all that you need to be new and improved
It's God's gift to you, it's God's gift to me

When Paw Paw stocked his grocery shelves he insisted on the best
So everything he ordered in had to pass the test
He was not afraid to try new things even tho' it'd mean he'd have to change
So detergent with a towel inside made its way to Paw Paw's store
And that ole' red Coca-Cola chest would one day be no more
There were beans and corn and cereal whose labels read New & Improved

Chorus

Well I miss Maw Maw and Paw Paw and the stories that they told
But they gave their hearts to Jesus, so they're walking streets of gold
And I know that they're together now in a place that's New and
Improved

APPENDIX F

Conversation and Activity Starters

Playing with your grandchild can teach life lessons along the way, like honesty, humility, sharing, competition, cooperation, taking turns, winning gracefully, and losing gracefully. Play is a wonderful way to experience amazing lessons for life without devastation consequences

The time you spend with them is precious and can be filled with wonder and delight or can be tense and uncomfortable. It can help to think ahead a bit and be prepared with age and location appropriate ideas and take into consideration your level of physical ability, of how to spend your time together

Things to talk about

Your family—who and how many, and growing up

Rules you had to obey growing up

Where you lived

Who you wanted to be like and who they want to be like

What you did with your friends at their age, what they do with theirs

Your school stories at their age

Stories of your own grandparents, where they lived and how

Your travels—road trips, exotic places, vacations

Stories of your mistakes at their age like eating too much ____ and got a tummy ache

What you wanted to be when you grew up and why

What they might want to be and why

Make up stories together about a dog, the tree in the front yard, and when the alien landed

Stories of "new technology" growing up like VCRs and dial up internet

Stories from the Bible—Noah, Jonah, Daniel and the lion's den

Characters in the Bible—what they did right or wrong

A movie you both saw

What their parents were like at their age

Ask if there's something on their mind they want to ask you or talk about!

Things to do together inside

Sing softly and rock in a chair
Wear a shawl or get a throw and drape it over the two of you
Make homemade ice cream and eat some together
Look at photos of the family—you at their age, their parents at their age
Read a book out loud with animated voices
Let them "read" a book or tell you the story from the pictures
Play cards or dominos
String buttons on a long thread with a needle, then tie together to make a necklace
Build or paint a model together, planes, cars, soldiers
Do age appropriate Science Kits or Projects
Play a board game—many teach life lessons about winning, losing
Share a collection you have and how you came to make it
Eat a meal at the table—no screens allowed
Make something to eat together, then enjoy it
Make breakfast and enjoy it—extra points for pancakes or waffles
Play dress up with old hats, shoes, shirts, gloves, costume jewelry, a purse or backpack they can fill with items and have a Fashion Show—extra points—Take pictures!
Make popcorn and watch a movie together—extra points for Jiffy Pop or popped in a pan or hot air popper—or for a movie with godly values
Bake cookies
Lick attack by a friendly dog
Make lemonade with real lemons and sip some
Build a fort—easy to drape a sheet/bedspread over the dining room table and chairs—face chairs outward and pull out for more room
Let them teach you how to play a game they like
Age appropriate jigsaw puzzles
Sing songs together, make up some silly ones
Make s'mores in the microwave
Dance party with music!—every 60 seconds change from the floor to the couch
Read age appropriate books together on a lazy afternoon or at bedtime
Sleepover with meals, movies, and snuggles
Bake together and enjoy the smells

Have a snack or Tea Party with dishes just their size
Let them "help" you do grown-up things
Say prayers
Ask what they want to do and do it!

Things to do together outside

Take a walk or hike and fill your pockets with pretty rocks, leaves
Play with a garden hose—water a lawn, garden, or sidewalk for fun
Run back and forth through the lawn sprinklers
Roll down a steep, grassy hill
Climb a tree
Swing from a tree swing
Push them on a swing set
Catch fireflies in a jar, then let them go
Rake leaves together and let them jump into the pile
Watch a lightning storm in the distance
Walk in the rain—umbrellas optional
Jump and splash in puddles
Hunt for earthworms
Make "Mud Pies" and bake them in the sun—Uhm, just don't eat.
Lay on a blanket and look at the clouds—share what they look like
Build a kite together, then go fly it
Draw on the sidewalk with chalk
Walk in the neighborhood and point out birds or trees you recognize
Pick flowers or vegetables from your garden
Pick up the fruit or nuts from your trees
Ride in an old Classic car
Take a nap together on a porch or by the pool or with a sleepy dog
Help give a dog a bath
Wrestle with a friendly dog
Catch snowflakes on your tongue
Make snow angels
Feed farm animals—ducks and chickens extra credit
Fill the bird feeders and birdbath and hummingbird feeder
Make "sun tea" and sip some in the shade
Pitch a tent and sleep out in the backyard
Play an outdoor lawn game like badminton, croquet, or horseshoes
Build a fort
Make s'mores over a fire

Go fishing—let them hold the slimy fish you all catch

Let them sit on your lap while you drive the mower, tractor, etc

Slip 'n Slide

Wash your car—especially if it's a cool car—then go for a ride

Work in the garden together—pull weeds, plant, fertilize

Clean the pool together

Spread a blanket and have a picnic

Pick berries

Go on a bike hike

Go on a night walk to check out the moon and stars

Use a telescope

Ask what they want to do and do it!

Places to go

Visit a library—show them where to find books at their level—sit on the poofy pillows and read one

A Carnival—go on one ride together and eat one fun food—caramel apple, caramel corn, cotton candy, funnel cake

Any lake or beach—wade in the water, chase the waves, collect shells, make a sand castle, and if they have them—do Paddleboats!

Any mountain trail to hike or woods to walk in

A ski slope to ski or snowboard together

Baseball games—professional or local teams, eat one fun food and cheer loudly

Ice Cream Parlor—share a banana split or Sundae, or get cones

A National Park, maybe camping or driving through

Go to church together

A petting zoo with baby animals—lambs, kids, colts

Ride a bus somewhere

A Thrift Store—how to spot a bargain

Somewhere they can play with new puppies

Place where there's a rope swing over water

A Craft Fair

A Farmer's Market

A Parade

An Air Show

A Rodeo

A Zoo

A Museum—Natural History, Art

The Dollar Store and give then $5, $10 or $20 to but whatever they want—amount by age

On a vacation to a Theme Park, stay in a hotel, eat out

Ask where they might want to go, and consider going

Things to teach your grandchild—How to:

Whistle with your fingers
Shoot marbles
Play jacks
Tie knots
Fold a proper paper airplane
Shuffle cards
Play Chopsticks on the piano
Use chopsticks
Hold and strum a guitar
Bait a hook
Catch a fish
Dive into a pool
Swim
Paddle a canoe or boat
Tell a joke
Make spaghetti
Make Mac 'n Cheese
Crack and scramble 2 eggs
Run the grill—hot dogs or chicken breasts to start
Whittle
Carve shapes in wood
Pitch a tent
Lay and start a 1-match fire
Change a tire
Simple self-defense moves
Dance moves—Moon walk, ballet, tap, or let them teach you
Strategy for a game you like
Knit, crochet, tat, macrame
Paint a model
Tie Dye
Make wax candles
Ride a bike, skateboard or scooter—helmet, knee and elbow pads
Anything you know how to do!

Things you can do for them

Display and praise their art work

Make a notebook or album of pictures of the two of you

Have a stool handy for them to use to be at your side

Play with them on their level

Write a special letter to them every year—Birthday or Christmas

Give gifts that reflect their interests

Instead of gifts, give experiences, like tickets to an event or performance, or family passes to a museum or zoo

Have extra diapers/supplies that might be needed when they come over

Have age appropriate books, toys, or videos for when they come to visit

Keep a journal of things you do together then at the end of the year write a letter remembering them saying how much you enjoyed the time you spent together

When you see or hear of great things others are doing with their grandchildren, write them down to make plans

Help them learn from their mistakes and know they are still loved

Tell them about Jesus again and again

Hold them when they need holding

Tell them you love them

Answer their ?? as best you can—they will probably forget the answers, but will remember how you took time for them

When they ask a million ?? and you don't know the answers, just listen

Understand when they are older and don't want to spend as much time with you, it doesn't mean they don't love you

Keep the lines of communication open so those spontaneous, meaningful conversations can happen at any time

Learn how to use your cell phone, computer or tablet to stay in touch

If you don't live close, call them, text, Zoom or Facetime with them

Send them a book that you both read and talk about it together on the phone or Zoom

Pray for God to guide you in your time together

Pray for their parents

Pray for them

APPENDIX G

Resources

♥ Legacy Coalition Website is legacycoalition.com

Legacy Coalition has weekly webinars, resources and events that help grandparents find purpose and have a greater spiritual impact on their grandchildren's lives.

Their website includes a blog, store, podcasts, radio episodes, Ask Dr. Joannie feedback on challenging issues, and a store with Bibles, books and DVDs

♥ www.christianbook.com is a website that offers toys, gifts, games for family nights, music, DVDs, books and Bibles at a discounted price

♥ Books:

A Grandmother's Prayers by Kay Swatkowski

The Christian Grandma's Idea Book by Ellen Banks Elwell

Quiet Moments for Grandmothers by Kay Marshall Strom

About the Authors

Eric Sprinkle: A former Whitewater Guide and Swift-water Rescue Instructor for the U.S. military, Eric travels the country speaking about the benefits of risk, managing fear, and how to make life more exciting by "living a slightly more dangerous lifestyle." If any of the book's images capture or inspire you? That's Jesus' fault for giving him traits like Risk-Taking, Daring, and being Adventurous.

Find more about him at AdventureExperience.net, including Speaker info, free book images, and an action-packed YouTube channel full of waterfalls, cliff faces, and whitewater silliness.

Laura Shaffer: An Army Brat moving almost every year till college, Laura was delighted to discover that wherever she went, God was always there ahead of her. Even though the houses, and friends changed, there was always Sunday School and church where she learned that God was always with her. And she felt it.

Her grandparents all lived in a small town in Texas, and although they didn't live close by, there were times; her first year and a half and seventh grade, they all lived in the same place. Then back in Texas for college, she and Maw Maw became close again. Her grandparents always made it clear they prayed for her, and their love and care had a great impact on her life.

It wasn't until recently she was blessed to become a grandmother. And praying for these blessings, their lives, their futures is something she can share with you now. This book can help you become intentional and consistent in your prayer life, which will deepen your relationship with God. So the prayers are for your precious grandchildren—the journey is for you!

Check out Laura's blog at www.DailyBiblePrayer.wordpress.com for scripture-based examples of her prayers anytime.

Additional Thoughts on Praying for Grandchildren

LOVE LAURA'S PRAYERS?

Looking for more from your new prayer partner Laura?

You've got it!

Have a look here for daily prayers, inspiring blogs, and more!

Check out her prayer blog—
www.dailyBibleprayer.wordpress.com

For her devotion blog—
www.hearmorefromGod.wordpress.com

Additional Thoughts on Praying for Grandchildren

Additional Thoughts on Praying for Grandchildren

More from Adventure Experience Press

Adventure Devos: The first devotional written exclusively for men with a heart for Risk and Danger

Adventure Devos: Women's Edition: An exciting devotional written exclusively for women with a Heart for Risk and Adventure

Adventure Devos: Youth Edition: Summer Camp never has to end when your devotional takes you adventuring all year long!

"Adventure Devos will challenge any man to be a better father or husband in no time, no doubt about it. Just read a few of the book's "Dares" and see for yourself how easily this devotional will get anyone into applying God's Word.

Megan "Katniss" Autrey, Colorado Certified Whitewater Guide Instructor, Wife and Mother

Additional Thoughts on Praying for Grandchildren

40DayPrayerGuides.com

Looking for another 40-Day Prayer Journey? Want to share and inspire others with stories from your last one? Welcome to the 40 Day Prayer Guide Series!

Be the first to download and check samples of the latest Guides, always weeks before they're listed for sale!

- Download free samples to share with friends
- Have a look at what's coming next in the 40-Day Prayer Guides series
- Share thoughts, ideas, and praises from your own 40-day journeys!

"This is a powerful book and is very much needed."

"I know several in my church right now who I plan to give copies to—real prayer warriors who would love this tool!" (Early Reader Feedback)

Come have a look, sign up for the Newsletter and be more inspired in your prayer life today!

Additional Thoughts on Praying for Grandchildren

Also available in the 40 Day Prayer Guide Series

40DayPrayerGuides.com

Ready-made prayers for someone's **Salvation, Blessings** for a friend, or asking for more **Godly Character**

THE PRAYERS ARE FOR THEM, THE JOURNEY IS FOR YOU

COMING SOON!

Praying for your **Pastor** and **Recovering from a Mistake** editions and much more! Grab one today!

Additional Thoughts on Praying for Grandchildren

Made in the USA
Middletown, DE
18 November 2022